READY SALTED

Peter Graystone

Scripture Union

© Peter Graystone 1998

First published 1998

Scripture Union, 207–209 Queensway, Bletchley,
Milton Keynes, MK2 2EB, England.

ISBN 1 85999 187 4

British Library Cataloguing-in-Publication Data. A catalogue
record of this book is available from the British Library.

Printed and bound in Great Britain by Cox & Wyman Ltd,
Reading.

Contents

Introduction   5

1   God – Father, Son and Spirit   7

2   Believing and belonging   24

3   The Christian life   36

4   The way of the world   51

5   Death and beyond   64

6   Church and worship   74

7   People and relationships   101

8   Money and possessions   113

9   Suffering and sadness   121

10   Hope and encouragement   130

11   Other points of view   136

Index   141

For Katy

Introduction

I've been keeping a commonplace book for ten years. It's on the table in front of me now – fat, red, spiral bound, with the back cover falling off and paste oozing out of two edges. In it I have scribbled down or stuck everything I have read or heard in the last decade that struck me as witty, wise or memorable.

I started it by accident! I bought the notebook to keep the minutes of a very boring committee of which I had found myself secretary. Driving home from the shop, I heard Michael Caine interviewed on the radio and he mentioned that he prayed regularly. It was exactly the kind of quotation I needed for a sermon I was going to preach the following Sunday, so I stopped the car and scribbled down what he had said while I still remembered it, on the only paper I had available. I was a useless committee secretary, and it is not surprising that the book was never used for its original purpose. Instead it has become priceless – to me at any rate! There are only two pages left blank in it now. The last entry is one I pasted in yesterday from a newspaper interview with Quentin Tarantino about film violence. The Michael Caine quote has found its way into the final selection for sentimental reasons; you are spared the Quentin Tarantino quote on the grounds of taste and decency!

Shortly after I started keeping the book, I was appointed editor of Scripture Union's worship and education scheme 'The SALT Programme'. Working on resources for adult and all-age worship, one of my tasks has been to provide preachers with illustrations to bring their sermons to life. For fifty-two weeks of every year during the last decade, the magazine has provided a basic 'recipe' to help church leaders begin their sermon preparation, and then anecdotes, jokes and quotations to add the 'flavour' which makes their Bible teaching engaging for the congregation – which makes it 'ready salted'! Virtually every word in this book appeared in 'SALT: all ages' first.

Not everything I scrawled down over the years has stood the test of time. Much from my commonplace book (and believe me, there is much!) no longer seems quite funny enough or wise enough for publication, or it has passed its quote-by date. The context in which something is said, or the personality of the person who says it, is often of more interest than the actual words. Memorable preachers know that for a comment by a little-known historical character to have an impact, it must be three times as good as if it was said by a Spice Girl. And no doubt even that reference will embarrass me when I read it again in a couple of years' time! So completing the book for its deadline has not been a matter of frantic writing, but of frantic deleting. I hope you find what is left funny, thought-provoking and useful, whether you are a speaker or just enjoy picking your way through compilations like these.

Thank you to Katy Davies, who typed and indexed the manuscript. Thank you to Alex, Gareth, Richard and Simon, who cut out the stories and spent a hilarious evening slapping them on the table in categories like an absurd card game. Thank you to the leaders of Emmanuel Church, South Croydon, where I have been privileged to share the teaching with two of the finest preachers in Britain today – James Jones and Rupert Higgins. And thank you to the congregation, who have so frequently found my sermons laughable!

Chapter 1

God – Father, Son and Spirit

1
Church Times, June 1996:
Correction: The phrase 'God can be temporary' in Tom Gardiner's review last week should have read 'God can be our contemporary'.

2
Liam Gallagher, lead singer of Oasis:
I won't change – not unless the geezer with the big beard lands down in front of me and pulls a giraffe out of his nostril and goes, 'I'm God.'

3
... and his brother, Noel Gallagher:
I would hope we mean more to people than putting money in a church basket and saying ten Hail Marys on a Sunday. Has God played Knebworth recently?

4
The artist formerly known as Prince:
God's a funky little dude, because everybody's looking for him and no one can find him.

5
*Woody Allen, film director, writing in **Without Feathers**:*
If only God would give me some clear sign! Like making a large deposit in my name at a Swiss bank.

6

The existence of God? Rather more believable than the alternative belief – that given enough time to develop, a lump of green slime can evolve into The Spice Girls... Hmm... Or maybe not!

7

The teleological argument, an ancient 'proof' of the existence of God first advanced by Aristotle and expanded in the thirteenth century by Thomas Aquinas – although both curiously omitted to mention U2:
If you have been walking alone for five days in a desert without seeing a living soul and you stumble upon a rock, you might well think to yourself, 'That rock is there by chance.' If, however, you stagger on alone and you come across a solar-powered compact disc player with full, graphically equalised stereo blasting out U2 records through top-of-the-range loudspeakers, you could be forgiven for thinking, 'That did not get there by accident; someone designed it and put it there.'

Which is the universe most like? The rock or the CD?

8

Fay Weldon, novelist:
Who cares about the half-second after the Big Bang! What about the half-second before?

9

Isaac Newton, seventeenth-century scientist:
In the absence of any other proof, the thumb alone would convince me of God's existence.

10

Meister Eckhardt, fourteenth-century Dominican monk:
God is like a person who clears his throat while hiding, and so gives himself away.

11

G K Chesterton, twentieth-century novelist:
When people stop believing in God, they do not come to believe in nothing; they start believing in anything.

12

Peter Graystone:
Some time ago I went on a preaching tour of Australia. One of the events was a family camp some two hours drive out of town, at which I was the speaker. The setting was a collection of shacks in a clearing deep within a magnificent forest. The politest description of it is 'primitive'. No electricity, basic sanitation, and my reward for travelling half way round the world was a semi-detached shack instead of a terraced shack! Swarthy Australian teenagers kept slapping me on the back and saying, 'Isn't this beaut, cobber! Bet you haven't got anything like this back in London!' I was able to answer, 'No, we haven't,' with unhesitating honesty!

I'm making fun of what was actually a terrific event! On the Saturday evening the lads came and asked me, 'Do you want to come out bivvying with us under the stars tonight?' Mishearing, and imagining that I had been invited to go out bevvying, I said yes. A few hours later I found myself lying under a blanket in the middle of nowhere questioning how I managed to get myself into this position, and wishing that my bed were twelve thousand miles nearer.

I had very little sleep, but I do remember being shaken awake just before dawn and sitting up with a start wondering what had happened to the ceiling. The reason they had woken me was that a family of kangaroos was standing closer to us than I had ever been to wild animals except in a zoo. We stood there looking at each other – a little line of men and a little line of kangaroos. And the sun came up red behind them. And it was... sensational!

I wondered who would be the first to try to put into words the awe we were all feeling. A sermon from me seemed the last thing that was needed! I was so surprised by what happened. A thirteen-year-old boy who had been aggressively uninterested in the spiritual part of the programme murmured, 'It looks like God's been here already.' I thought he was joking, so I smiled and turned to join in the joke. But catching sight of his face I realised that he was absolutely serious. And I had one of those wonderful moments when you think you are standing next to a teenager, and you suddenly realise that you are standing next to a believer.

13
Kenny Everett, one of BBC Radio 1's first disc jockeys, began his broadcast:
Isn't it gorgeous out there today? Aah! Good old God!

14
Julian of Norwich, fourteenth-century nun and writer:
And he showed me more, a little thing, the size of a hazelnut, on the palm of my hand, rounded like a ball. I looked at it thoughtfully and wondered, 'What is this?' And the answer came, 'It is all that is made.' I marvelled that it continued to exist and did not suddenly disintegrate; it was so small. And again my mind supplied the answer, 'It exists both now and forever, because God loves it.' In short, everything owes its existence to the love of God.

15
Karen Armstrong, writer:
Love can be a very frightening thing – love the raging fire, love the shock to the entire system, as well as the tender aspects of love. It's not a sort of mystical swooning, it's an electric shock. If a human being walked unprotected into God, he'd probably shrivel up.

16
*John Stott, writing in **Basic Christianity**:*
There is a hunger in the heart of man which none but God can satisfy; a vacuum which only God can fill.

17

Dag Hammarskjöld, Swedish statesman and first Secretary General of the United Nations:
God does not die on the day when we cease to believe in a personal deity, but we die on the day when our lives cease to be illumined by the steady radiance of a wonder, the source of which is beyond all reason.

18

Sister Wendy Beckett, nun, art critic and television presenter:
All experience of art is an indirect experience of God. I don't see why people couldn't get in touch with God through rap music, a real experience of something thrilling.

19

Rob Draper, twentieth-century preacher:
In the twilight of the gods, men came forth like giants. In the twilight of the men, all the gods came back again.

20

Barbara Ellen, writing in the **Observer***, March 1997:*
Who would have thought that God still had it in him to grab the headlines? Let's face it, he is deeply unfashionable right now. You could gift-wrap God in a big pink bow and give him away in a raffle and some people would still wish that they had won the sink tidy. But it works the other way too!

21

Iranaeus, second-century Bishop of Lyons:
God created man in order to have someone on whom to shower his love.

22

Professor Stephen Hawking, physicist, writing in **A Brief History of Time***:*
The usual approach of science constructing a mathematical model cannot answer the questions of *why* there should be a

universe for the model to describe ... If we find the answer to that, it would be the ultimate triumph of human reason – for then we would know the mind of God.

23
Sinead O'Connor, singer:
God is good; we've just messed it up. He's probably biting his nails right now, having a smoke thinking, 'What the hell am I gonna do now?'

24
At art college you are taught: 'Never rub out.' Instead you are taught to use whatever you have and work from it, no matter how unsatisfactory it may be as a starting point. This has eternally been God's approach to the way humans have used his perfect creation.

25
An advert in the **Bristol Evening Post**:
God's solution to world problems. A series of talks in the Quicksave Hall in Clevedon.

26
Sara Maitland, writing in the **Independent**, *May 1994:*
I see God as an exhausted but devoted mother wondering even at 3.30 am, when he said he would be in at midnight, if it is fair to emotionally blackmail her teenager with tears, or on the other hand never to let him out of the house again for the rest of his life.

   If she is sensible and affectionate, she is more likely to do the former than the latter, and I agree with her. Is God guilty? Not proven!

27
Peter Graystone:
Last week I was taken aback to see at the top of my supermarket receipt, 'Thank you, Mr Graystone, for shopping at

Tesco today.' My first reaction was: 'Good grief! They know my name!' My second was: 'Of course! They knew it from the store loyalty card which sends me discount vouchers.' My third was: 'Oh dear! That means they also have a record of whether my purchases included health food and the *Church Times*, or a bottle of gin and *Playboy*.'

If their computer knows all that, it is way beyond my imagination what the almighty Lord knows about me – name, loyalty, virtues and vices. Thank God for *his* free gift!

28

Peter Plouviez, General Secretary of the Actors' Union, on black Broadway star Ken Page's role in the short-lived musical Children of Eden:
British Equity welcomes talented foreign artists working in our country, even when they are required to play such an obviously British part as God.

29

A primary school class was doing a project as part of their religious education, and went on a trip to the local church. One boy loved exploring the building, and couldn't wait to get home and tell his family about it. He said to his grandmother, 'We went into God's house today. It was great!'
His grandmother was delighted and asked, with a twinkle in her eye, 'Did you see God?'

'No,' replied the boy seriously. 'But I did see his wife vacuuming the carpet.'

30

Ian Wilson, writing in Jesus: the Evidence:
With every sceptical faculty alive and kicking I *do* believe that nearly two thousand years ago, in the land we today call Israel, 'the Word' was made flesh and dwelt in a Galilean Jew called Jesus ... for a brief moment there was magic in the air, the sick were healed, and men and women caught a glimpse of heaven.

31

Josephus, first-century Jewish historian, writing about
Jesus:
It was at that time that a man appeared – if 'man' is the right
word – who had all the attributes of a man but seemed to be
something greater. His actions were superhuman, for he
worked such wonderful and amazing miracles that I for one
cannot regard him as a man; yet in view of his likeness to
ourselves, I cannot regard him as an angel either.

It is also stated that after his execution and entombment
he disappeared entirely. Some people actually assert that he
had risen; others retort that his friends stole him away. I for
one cannot decide where the truth lies.

32

Derek Nimmo, writing in **Oh Come on All Ye Faithful**:
Jesus said to them, 'Who do you say that I am?'

They replied, 'You are the eschatological manifestation
of the ground of our being, the kerygma of which we find the
ultimate meaning in our interpersonal relationships.'

And Jesus said, 'What?'

33

Karl Barth, one of the most influential theologians of the
twentieth century, was asked what he considered the most
profound theological truth he had taught in all his years of
advanced academic pursuit. After a pause, he replied:
Jesus loves me, this I know,
For the Bible tells me so.

34

In C S Lewis' allegory, **The Lion, the Witch and the**
Wardrobe, *the lion Aslan represents Jesus. Lucy, a young*
girl, is told about him by a beaver!:
'If there's anyone who can appear before Aslan without
their knees knocking, they're either braver than most or else
just silly.'

'Then isn't he safe?' said Lucy.
'Of course he isn't safe. But he's good!'

35

Patricia St John's novel **Star of Light** *has a vivid illustration of how Jesus, the light of the world, is at once a consolation and a discomfort. Hamid, a homeless boy in North Africa visits an English missionary-nurse. While she is out of the room he steals two eggs, then waits for her outside in the darkness and rain. The nurse brings a lamp out to help them on their journey through the night. She invites Hamid to come under her cloak so that both can walk in the light. He won't! He prefers to shuffle against the wall, slipping around in the mud, out of the light's range. Finally, he misses his step in the darkness, falls, and breaks the eggs he was clutching. The nurse brings the lamp over to him and all is revealed. She takes him home, cleans him up and bandages his knees, saying:*

Hamid, you fell and hurt yourself because you wouldn't walk in the light. You were afraid of it because you'd stolen my eggs. You couldn't walk with me in the light because you'd done wrong... I'm going to forgive you – but promise you won't steal from my house again.

36

Peter Graystone:
So God looks at his own earth ruined and says, 'What can be done?' But from the depths of time eternal he already knows what has to be done. He reaches for a *Benetton* sweater, he slips on a pair of *Levi* jeans and *Marks and Spencer* socks, and he says, 'OK. I'll go!' And there he is, walking down Oxford Street among us.

If it is true that Jesus Christ is God, then he has conferred on the human body more dignity than can possibly be conceived. It has become a temple.

37

Joan Osborne's 1996 world-wide hit was titled:
What if God was one of us?

38

A little boy was drawing a picture with great concentration. 'What are you doing?' asked his mum.

'I'm drawing a picture of Jesus,' he replied.

His mum did not quite know how to respond. She queried, 'But no one knows what Jesus looked like.'

'They will when I've finished this picture.'

39

Clifford Stewart, North American evangelist:
I sent my parents a microwave oven last Christmas. They were excited that now they too would be part of the instant generation. When Dad unpacked the microwave and plugged it in, literally within seconds the microwave transformed two smiles into two frowns! Even after reading the directions they could not make it work.

Two days later my mother was playing bridge with a friend and confessed her inability to get the oven even to boil water. The friend offered to lend her a better book of instructions. 'I don't need better instructions to get the darned thing to work,' she exclaimed. 'What I really need is my son to come along with the gift.'

40

Glenn Hoddle, manager of the England football team:
I went to Israel to play for England. We were taken to Bethlehem to see the birthplace of Jesus. Up to that point for me Jesus was just a story. But when I saw where he had lived, I can only say that I had an inner conviction that the story was true. When I went back home I started to read the Bible and talk to some Christians... I found answers to questions I was asking... Jesus came to show us that God really does love us and Christ has given us the chance to find out what life is all about.

41

Milton Jones, winner of the 1996 Perrier Award for the best newcomer in comedy:
The traditional face of Christ is that of a depressed Bee Gee. This belies his superhumanity. I'm sure he could shed tears of sadness and yet also laughed longer and louder than anyone else.

42

C S Lewis, writing in **Mere Christianity:**
A man who was merely a man and said the sort of thing Jesus said would not be a great moral teacher. He would either be a lunatic – on a level with the man who says he is a poached egg – or else he would be the Devil of Hell. You must make your choice. Either this man was and is, the Son of God, or else a madman or something worse... Let us not come with any patronising nonsense about his being a great human teacher. He has not left that open to us. He never intended to!

43

Madonna, singer and actress:
When I was growing up I was religious in a passionate way. Jesus Christ was like a movie star, my favourite idol of all.

44

The late, great John Wayne played the centurion who crucified Jesus in the film *The Greatest Story Ever Told*. He only had about a dozen words, but they included the climactic, 'Truly, this was the Son of God.'

Story has it that the director was not thrilled with the way his words drawled out through his thick American accent, and pleaded, 'Put some awe into it, John.'

So they did a retake of the scene with Wayne intoning, 'Awe truly, this was the Son of God.'

45

Sir Cliff Richard, singer:
During those extraordinary minutes of history, Jesus, who had no sin of his own and could therefore be absolutely at one and in harmony with his Father, took on the sin of the whole of humanity ... I'm only grateful, and want my life to be a thank you to the God who now accepts me ... because Jesus paid for the slate to be wiped clean.

46

Every Christmas, the borough council of Croydon, South London, leaves on some of the lights of its skyscraper offices overnight so that they illuminate the shape of a cross. This bright cross stands out for miles and miles across the surrounding hills. Letters to the local papers show that some are infuriated by it; others take strength from its dominance over the town. It is indeed, in the words of 1 Corinthians 1:18, 'nonsense to those who are being lost; but for us who are being saved it is God's power'.

47

Superstitions about the cross are rife. Those who wear one as a good luck charm miss its true value completely. However, to refuse to wear one because it is an instrument of execution ('You wouldn't wear an electric chair!') is equally superstitious in another way. Some, ridiculously, shelter from lightning under an elder tree since they think it was the wood of the cross and affords them protection. One man crosses himself as he leaves home to go to work as an entirely pragmatic safety check: 'Glasses, flies, wallet, filofax'!

48

Peter Graystone:
When I went to stay at the home of my five-year-old niece she was bursting to tell me about a prayer she had learnt at school. 'You say it,' I smiled encouragingly, 'and I'll repeat it.'

'Well,' she replied thoughtfully, 'it's more of a prayer that you do than a prayer that you say.' And she slowly and reverently crossed herself with the words, 'From my head to my toes, from my shoulder to my shoulder, I love you Lord Jesus.'

49

I asked Jesus: 'How much do you love me?'

'This much,' he answered, and he stretched wide his arms and died.

50

At All Saints', Hordle, in Hampshire, after a performance of Stainer's *Crucifixion*, the choirmaster put up a notice in the choir vestry: 'The Crucifixion – well done everybody!' By the end of the day, someone had added: 'The Resurrection – well done God!'

51

1978 was the extraordinary year of three popes. Karol Wotjyla was elected Pope John Paul II in succession to John Paul I, who died tragically after only a few months as pontiff. The *Daily Express* had the most remarkable headline: 'Pope Dies Again.'

That is one headline which could not possibly apply to Jesus!

52

In the melting-pot of philosophical thinking that followed the French Revolution, a young man attempted to establish a new religion. It was, he declared, a considerable improvement on Christianity – but it obstinately refused to get off the ground. The man found himself in conversation with the statesman Charles-Maurice de Talleyrand, a leading thinker of his day. 'Starting a new religion is more difficult than I and my supporters thought,' he explained. 'Do you have any advice?'

Talleyrand protested that he hardly knew what to recommend. 'But there is one plan which you might at least try. I advise you to be crucified, and to rise again on the third day.'

53

Thomas Carlyle, nineteenth-century Scottish historian:
If Jesus Christ were to come today, people would not crucify him. They would ask him to dinner, and hear what he had to say, and make fun of it.

54

Desmond Morris, anthropologist:
One day, when I was writing a book, the doorbell rang. At the door was an enormous man. Around his neck was a cardboard plaque with 'I am come again' written on it.

'I am Jesus,' he said. 'I am come again.'

'I'm sorry,' I replied. 'I'm terribly busy.'

'That's what they said last time,' he answered, and wandered away.

55

Sue Clutterham, infant school teacher:
The mother of a seven-year-old in my class came to me after school and said: 'Excuse me, but have you been talking about Jesus' second coming?' I had!

'I'm delighted,' she went on. 'But perhaps you could explain a little more because she has just told me excitedly that he's coming down the chimney this year with Santa Claus.'

56

*Woody Allen, in the film **Hannah and her Sisters**:*
If Jesus Christ came back to earth today, he'd never stop throwing up at the things people do in his name.

57

A family was on holiday in a remote cottage in North Wales – no electricity, no water, gas only from camping stoves. At bedtime the young daughter was extremely brave about going upstairs with her mother by the light of a candle. She became fearful only when a draught blew through the bedroom door and the candle went out, leaving them in total darkness.

'I'm going back downstairs to get the matches,' said the mother, 'but you need not be afraid, because Jesus is here with you.'

'Oh dear,' replied the daughter. 'Couldn't you stay here and we'll send Jesus for the matches?'

58

In Greek mythology, one of the labours of Hercules was to clean the stables of Augeas. In them Augeas had stabled three thousand head of oxen for thirty years, without once cleaning them out. It was Hercules' task to clear away the vast accumulation of filth. He did not even attempt to do it himself. He diverted the course of two rivers so that they flowed through the stables, and their cleansing power did what no human effort could have done!

The Holy Spirit links humans with a power far greater than their own, and that flood tide of cleansing and renewing does for us what we ourselves could never do.

59

Peter Graystone:
In my worst nightmare I am walking home from the shops, and as I turn the corner I see to my horror that my flat is on fire. I reach down into my dressing gown pocket (don't ask me why I'm wearing a dressing gown to the shops in this dream – goodness knows what Freud would make of it) and from it I take a water pistol. Frantically I start squirting little dribbles into the furnace which has by now engulfed the whole block.

Then from behind me I hear the familiar siren of a fire engine, and before I know what is going on, a mighty torrent of water hurtles over my shoulder. It gathers up all the pathetic droplets from my water pistol and thunders them with awesome force straight into the heart of the fire.

That is what the Holy Spirit is doing with my words and thoughts when I begin to pray.

60

Carlo Carretto, twentieth-century writer and monk:
We are the wire; the Holy Spirit is the current. Our only power is to let the current pass through us.

61

Agnes Sanford, writing in **Healing Gifts of the Spirit***:*
The Holy Spirit, who is the giver of the gift of healing, simply cannot be circumscribed within the walls of a church. He cannot abide it and he will not, but will dim his power in any church that dares to claim him as the exclusive tool of the clergy. For indeed the healing spirit of God is in the wind and the sun and the little creeping things upon the earth and is most certainly available to the one who prays with faith, be he minister or layperson – man, woman or child.

62

D L Moody, the nineteenth-century North American evangelist, when asked whether he was filled with the Holy Spirit:
Yes, but I leak a little.

63

Corrie Ten Boom, writer and survivor of a Nazi concentration camp:
I have a glove here in my hand. The glove cannot do anything

by itself but, when my hand is in it, can do many things. True, it is not the glove, but my hand in the glove that acts.

We are gloves. It is the Holy Spirit in us who is the hand, who does the job. We have to make room for the hand so that every finger is filled.

64

John Wesley, eighteenth-century evangelist and founder of Methodism:
Tell me how it is that in this room there are three candles and but one light, and I will explain to you the mode of divine existence.

And finally...

65

A riddle about the Trinity:
The head waiter greeted a man as he walked into a restaurant: 'Who will be dining with you tonight?'

'My sister's brother, my wife's husband and my son's father,' replied the man.

The waiter led him to a table for one.

Chapter 2

Believing and belonging

66

A woman arrived at the gates of heaven and flung herself on her knees: 'Forgive me, forgive me, O how I need forgiveness.'

A stern and imposing figure bent down toward her. 'Why do you plead for mercy in such a way?'

'I have lived the last decade as a cheat and a fraud,' sobbed the woman.

'I see you come from England,' observed the saint.

'Yes,' she replied. 'I've lived all my life in St Ives. I'm so proud of my beautiful town. That's been the problem!'

'Tell me what is troubling your soul.'

'Every year for the last ten years, St Ives has been entered in the Beautiful Britain competition to find the loveliest town in the country. And for each one of those years, I have sneaked round to the other shortlisted towns on the day of the final. I've dropped a bit of litter here. I've kicked over a flower pot there. I've sounded my car hooter in the most peaceful places. And that's how St Ives has come to win the award for most beautiful town in Britain ten times in a row. O have mercy on me, I need to be forgiven.'

And a compassionate voice replied, 'Don't you worry, my dear. You are just the sort of person we want in heaven.' The woman's whole demeanour changed. 'I had no idea forgiveness was so easy to find. Thank you, St Peter, thank you.' And as the gates swung wide and she walked through she heard a voice behind her, 'Actually, I'm not St Peter. He's having his lunch break.'

'Who are you then?' asked the woman.

'I'm St Ive.'

67

The bishop's car ran out of petrol, but much to his relief his wife remembered passing a garage half a mile back down the road. He searched the boot for a container, but he could only find his baby grandson's potty, so it had to do! He trudged to the petrol station, then back with a full container.

The leader of a new church, driving by, recognised a fellow Christian in need and stopped his car to offer help. As he approached he saw the bishop pour the contents of the potty into the tank. The man gasped: 'If I'd known they had faith like that in the Church of England I'd never have left!'

68

The North American Douglas Coupland is one of the most significant young writers in the world. In **Generation X** *he named and described an entire generation – the 'twenty-something' recession-hit subculture of men and women who opted out of committed involvement in anything. It was an enormously impressive and influential book, and Coupland became a spokesman for his age. His second book,* **Life After God** *is even better-written. At some point in the narrative he explains that he has a secret to tell us, but he won't reveal it until the moment is right.*

Toward the end, he goes up into the mountains, takes off his clothes and swims in an ice-cold pool under a waterfall. In the roar of the water he hears a roar of clapping hands as if the whole of nature is urging him to seek wholeness. And then, so unexpected that you have to read it twice to check you are not imagining it, he writes this:

Now – here is my secret: I tell it to you with an openness of heart that I doubt I shall ever achieve again, so I pray that you are in a quiet room as you hear these words. My secret is that I need God – that I am sick and can no longer make it alone. I need God to help me give, because I no longer seem to be capable of giving; to help me be kind, as I no longer seem capable of kindness; to help me love, as I seem beyond being able to love.

69

Peter Graystone:
Having a religion is becoming more and more acceptable. It's like underwear! Twenty years ago it was personal, close to you, and you never talked about it. Nowadays men deliberately wear their trousers loose enough for the labels to be on show. In fact it has become admirable to have a spiritual foundation. Just so long as you don't try to persuade someone that your *St Michaels* are a better foundation than their *Calvin Kleins*!

70

A father was reading a bedtime story to his son, a fantasy full of impossible adventure. When he had finished, the boy asked his dad, 'Does every fairy story start with the words: "Once upon a time, long, long ago"?'

His dad wearily replied, 'No. I once heard one which began: "When you become a Christian all your problems will come to an end."'

71

In the nineteenth-century, the publishers Harper and Rowe had a horse called Dobbin who operated their printing press, tied to a pole and walking round and round in circles. In old age, it was decided that he had earned his freedom. He was uncoupled from the machine, taken to some glorious countryside, and set loose in a field.

The poor animal rapidly declined.

In a rush of sentiment, the board met to decide what to do with the ailing horse. Someone had an idea. A pole was erected in the field and the horse was tied to it. Dobbin began to walk round and round again. Within days he had returned to full health.

How sad that no one had given him a taste of freedom before it was too late!

72

The Shorter Catechism of the Westminster Assembly, 1644:
Question: What is the chief end of man?
Answer: Man's chief end is to glorify God, and to enjoy him for ever.

73

Astronomer: Why do you make religion so complicated? When it boils down to it, it's just 'Love your neighbour as yourself.'

Theologian: I know what you mean. I often wonder why you make science so complicated. When it boils down to it, it's just: 'Twinkle, twinkle, little star.'

74

In Douglas Adams' cult best-seller **The Hitch-hiker's Guide to the Galaxy,** the scientists build a hyper-computer in order to work out the ultimate answer to life, the universe and everything. It takes several million years, and when it has come up with the answer it declares, 'You're not going to like it!' They persist anyway, and programme it to print out the answer. It is: 'Forty-two!'

Disappointed with the simplicity, they build another computer to find out: 'If that is the ultimate answer, what is the ultimate question?' This too takes thousands of lifetimes before a report is ready. Finally it prints out the ultimate question of life, the universe and everything. It is: 'What is six times eight?' After all those millions of years of struggle, it had got the answer wrong!

75

John Polkinghorne, scientist and President of Queen's College, Cambridge, on being asked whether his Christian

beliefs would be changed if intelligent life were found on another planet:
If little green men on Mars need saving, then God will take little green flesh.

76

Celia Haddon, editor of the health and sex guide **The Sunday Times Book of Body Maintenance:**
I needed, desperately needed, some help and comfort in my attempt to lead a good life. Christ seemed to offer that support. But if I had waited to be convinced by the weight of historical argument or by the logic of theological dogma, I should be godless still.

77

Andre Agassi, tennis player:
I knew there had to be more important things than tennis or money. So I thought I'd give Jesus a chance. There are only two directions in life – one that leads to helping others and one that leads to selfish purposes. I wasn't on my way to helping others. What Christianity has offered me is peace of mind and the understanding that it's not a big deal if you get beat.

78

George Gallup, founder of the Gallup polling organisation:
We revere the Bible, but don't read it. We think the ten commandments are valid rules for living, but we can't name them. [According to my polling company] 13 per cent of the North American population have a deeply transforming faith... I am a person who loves Jesus Christ, and who stumbles along in Christ's path, and tries to live up to what Christ is calling us to do and to be.

79

Judy Simpson, heptathlete, aka Nightshade of the Gladiators, who became a Christian at the Olympic games in Seoul, writing in Christians in Sport magazine:
I was sharing a room with Loreen Hall. I noticed that she used to pray in the morning and before she went to bed. One night I was feeling so bored I went along to a meeting of Christian athletes. As I sat and listened, I was impressed that they were so committed and so genuine. It was just the way they lived their lives. The lack of malicious gossip about anyone else was a shining witness for what having Christ in your life could do. That really spoke to me. I committed my life.

80

Gavin Peacock, Chelsea footballer, interviewed in the Guardian about whether being a Christian had made him a better player:
Well, God hasn't given me an extra yard of space, which would be handy, but he has guided me in my career, helping me with all the decisions I've made. He gave me the talents to be a footballer, and as a Christian I realise that you have to maximise the use of the talents you've been given to glorify him. My faith has helped me to relax, get things in perspective, handle the ups and downs, so it has made me a better player in that sense.

81

Malcolm Muggeridge, twentieth-century journalist and broadcaster:
I may, I suppose, regard myself as a relatively successful man. People occasionally stare at me in the streets; that's fame. I can earn enough to qualify for admission to the higher slopes of the Inland Revenue; that's success. It might happen once in a while that something I said or wrote was sufficiently heeded for me to persuade myself that it represented a serious impact on our time; that's fulfilment. Yet I say to you and beg you to believe me, multiply these tiny triumphs by a

million, add them all together, and they are nothing, less than nothing, a positive impediment, measured against one draught of that living water Christ offers to the spiritually thirsty irrespective of who or what they are.

82

David Jenkins, former (and controversial) Bishop of Durham, on a decision at the age of twelve to dedicate his life to Christ:
I can still see the bearded preacher on the platform in Bromley saying something like, 'Here is God who has sent his Son to rescue you from your sins, and you must respond.' And I can remember when saying my prayers in bed that night, thinking to myself, 'This will be like a New Year resolution; it will wear off.' But then something said to me, 'No it won't,' and – well, it didn't wear off. It never has worn off.

83

The **Observer**, *September 1990:*
So far no national newspaper editor has been 'reborn'. The *Independent* put out a flier last week describing *News of the World* editor Patsy Chapman as 'an ardent Christian'. Not true, she says, adding: 'I consulted a lawyer, but he said it wasn't actionable'.

84

C S Lewis, twentieth-century academic and writer, on his conversion:
I chose, yet it did not really seem possible to do the opposite. It was the relentless pursuit by the mouse of the cat!

85

C S Lewis, writing in **Surprised by Joy**:
A young man who wishes to remain a sound atheist cannot be too careful of his reading.

86

Words from the Jewish ghetto in Warsaw, in about 1940:
I believe in the sun, even when it's not shining;
I believe in love, even when I cannot feel it;
I believe in God, even when he is silent.

87

Hugh Latimer, martyred Bishop of Winchester, written from prison in 1555:
Pardon me and pray for me; pray for me I say. For I am sometimes so fearful, that I would creep into a mousehole; sometimes God doth visit me again with his comfort. So he cometh and goeth.

88

Woody Allen, film director:
I am plagued by doubts. What if everything is an illusion and nothing exists? In that case I definitely overpaid for my carpet.

89

Dorothy Parker, North American humorist, in a poem called **Inventory**:
Four be the things I'd been better without:
Love, curiosity, freckles and doubt.

90

George MacDonald, nineteenth-century Scottish novelist:
Doubts are the messengers of the living one to the honest.

91

Graffiti from a London wall:
Unbelief is the darkness in which we develop our negatives.

92

Bob Dylan, singer, from the album **Slow Train Coming**:
You gotta serve somebody;

You gotta serve somebody;
Well, it may be the devil or it may be the Lord,
But you gonna have to serve somebody.

93

Bono, lead singer of U2:
All I've got is a red guitar, three chords and the truth - the rest is up to you.

94

Garibaldi, the nineteenth-century Italian patriot, to his soldiers:
What I have to offer you is fatigue, danger, struggle and death; the chill of the cold night in the free air and heat under the burning sun; no lodgings, no provisions, but forced marches, dangerous watchposts, continued struggles. Those who love freedom and their countryman follow me.

95

Ralph Waldo Emerson, nineteenth-century North American poet:
All I have seen leads me to trust the Creator for all I have not seen.

96

Colonel James Irwin, Apollo astronaut:
We live in a world with a withered sense of wonder.

97

St Augustine of Hippo, fourth-century African bishop:
How late I came to love you, O beauty so ancient and so fresh, how late I came to love you! You were within me while I had gone outside to seek you ... Always you were with me, and I was not with you ... You called, you cried, you shattered my deafness. You sparkled, you blazed, you drove away my blindness. You shed your fragrance, and I drew in my breath, and I pant for you. I tasted and now I hunger and

thirst. You touched me, and now I burn with longing for
your peace.

98

*Charles de Foucauld, (Brother Charles of Jesus), the French
explorer and hermit, writing at the start of the twentieth
century:*
Father, I abandon myself into your hands; do with me what
you will. Whatever you may do, I thank you; I am ready for
all, I accept all. Let only your will be done in me, and in all
your creatures – I wish no more than this, Lord.

Into your hands I commend my soul; I offer it to you
with all the love of my heart. For I love you, Lord, and so
need to give myself, to surrender myself into your hands,
without reserve, and with boundless confidence. For you are
my Father!

99

*Ignatius of Loyola, sixteenth-century founder of the Society
of Jesus:*
Take, Lord, and receive all my liberty, my memory, my
understanding, and my entire will, all that I have and possess.
Thou hast given it all to me. To thee, O Lord, I return it. All
is thine, dispose of it wholly according to thy will. Give me
thy love and thy grace, for this is sufficient for me.

100

*Dag Hammarskjöld, first Secretary General of the United
Nations, writing in **Markings**:*
Thou takest the pen – and the lines dance;
Thou takest the flute – and the notes shimmer;
Thou takest the brush – and the colours sing;
So all things have meaning and beauty in that space beyond
time where thou art;
How then can I hold back anything from thee?

101

C S Lewis, writing in **Mere Christianity***:*
You never know how much you really believe anything until
its truth becomes a matter of life and death to you.

102

Maurice Nassan, writer:
A friend went to stay in Cornwall. One afternoon he went
for a walk and got lost. As evening drew on he grew more
and more afraid of falling into a disused mineshaft, but it
was too cold to sit down, so he kept going. Inevitably, he
missed his footing, slipped and began to slither down into a
pit. He managed to grab on to a rock. He was able to hang
on for about twenty minutes, but the agony in his arms grew
so great that he knew he would soon have to let go and
plunge to his death.

He was about to let go when he saw, to his immense
relief, a little light in the distance which began to grow
greater and he knew that help was coming. He shouted loud
with all the energy he had left. When the rescuers arrived and
shone their light down on him the first thing they saw was
that his feet were dangling within a foot of solid earth. This
mineshaft had been filled in!

103

Bruce Larson, writing in **Edge of Adventure***:*
In the middle of a lonely trail across the Amargosa Desert in
the USA was an old pump. It was the only source of drinking water and travellers might be in a desperate state by the
time they reached it under the baking sun. Attached to the
pump handle was a letter:

'This pump is all right as of June 1932. I put a new
leather sucker washer into it and it ought to last several
years. But this leather washer dries out and the pump has got
to be primed. Under the white rock I buried a bottle of water.
There's enough water in it to prime the pump, but not if you
drink some first. Pour in about one quarter and let her soak

to wet the leather. Then pour in the rest, medium fast, and pump like crazy. You'll get water. The well has never run dry. Have faith. When you get watered up, fill the bottle and put it back like you find it for the next fellow.

Signed Desert Pete.

PS Don't go drinking up the water first. Prime the pump with it first and you'll get all you can hold.

And finally...

104

A man fell over a cliff and, as he tumbled down the sheer drop, managed to grab on to a scrubby bush growing from the side of the rock. Terrified, he hung in space, his life flashing before him. In desperation, he shouted toward heaven, 'Is there anyone up there?'

To his astonished delight, a voice floated down: 'I am the Lord God, and I am here.'

'What should I do?' called the man.

The voice replied, 'Let go of the branch and, with my protection, you will float harmlessly down to the beach below.'

The man glanced under his feet to the jagged rocks at the foot of the cliff, hundreds of metres below. He gulped, and looked back toward heaven. 'Well... is there anyone else up there?'

Chapter 3

The Christian Life

105

A churchwarden arrived at a vicarage to keep his appointment with the vicar, but his teenage son answered the door. 'I'm afraid he won't be able to see you after all. He's just had a letter offering him the post of Bishop of the Bahamas!'

'But he's only just been appointed to this parish.'

'Yes, but he's being offered a car, six weeks' annual holiday and twice the salary. So he's gone to his study to pray for guidance.'

'Is your mother praying with him?'

'No, she's up in the bedroom packing the suitcases.'

106

Someone I met told me that he was absolutely convinced that God wanted him to go and work as a missionary in South America. When I asked him why, he explained that he had been eating a chocolate bar while he was praying, and he suddenly realised that it was full of Brazil nuts. My only thought was, thank goodness it wasn't a *Mars* bar!

107

Rob Frost, evangelist:

In France one night in a torrential thunderstorm, when I was completely lost, I came across a signpost at a road junction. It read to the left: 'Toutes directions', and to the right: 'Toutes autres directions'.

Sometimes, God's guidance can seem just as confusing.

108

There is something about the human need for forgiveness which is inclined to bring out a rash of misprints in newspapers. How else do you explain these?:

From the **Chichester Evening News***:* Miss Hampshire ... is friendly, likeable, and easy to talk to. She has a fine, fair skin, which she admits ruefully comes out in freckles at the first hint of sin.

Or this from the **Dublin Evening Herald***:* Fifteen churches have been closed in Dublin City because of swindling congregations.

From the **Yorkshire Post***:* Patricia Middleton sang 'Christians dost thou see them?' at the close of Sunday night's service. Miss Middleton is a qualified vice instructor.

Or, even worse, from the **Croydon Advertiser***:* Born to Rev and Mrs David Wilson of St James' Church, a git of a son.

109

John Carlin, writing in **The Independent***, May 1997:*

In a stunning act of repentance, South Africa's Dutch Reformed Church formally declared apartheid to be a sin, and confessed its guilt for the suffering and injustice caused in the name of racial separateness. After Professor Potgieter had spoken, Archbishop Desmond Tutu had half his audience in tears when he replied: 'God has brought us to this moment and I just want to say to you: I cannot, when someone says "Forgive me," say, "I do not".'

110

Terry Anderson, longest-held of the Western hostages imprisoned in Beirut during the 1980s:

I am a Christian and a Catholic... It is required of me to forgive, no matter how hard it is. I am determined to do that.

111

*Marley's ghost in Charles Dickens' novel **A Christmas Carol**:*
We must not drag the chain of the past with us wherever we go.

112

The Inland Revenue received a letter from a man who, after converting to Christianity, was reconsidering his life:
I am having sleepless nights because of the burden of my past. I am therefore enclosing £100 which I forgot to declare.
PS If I still can't get to sleep I will send the rest.

113

*P J O'Rourke, writing in **Age and Guile**:*
There must be a lot of sin in Arkansas to support this much forgiveness. All sorts of Christian enterprises advertise on the radio shows. There are Christian bookstores, Christian day care centres, Christian drug and alcohol counselling centres. For all I know there are Christian strip joints. The girls don't disrobe. They don't dance or wear make-up either. I mean, this is Baptist territory! They sit in pews and take their clothes off in their hearts.

114

*A senior demon to his young nephew in C S Lewis' **The Screwtape Letters**:*
No one knows how bad he is until he has tried to be good. There is a silly idea about that good people don't know what temptation means.

115

Peter Graystone:
When I was young, before the days of widespread central heating, my grandparents lived in a house that was heated by coal fires. The fireplace in their front room was splendid, and the most magnificent feature of it was a large brass knob toward the bottom. (I think its function was to make it easy

to pull out the grate with a pair of tongs.)

My grandparents impressed upon me time and time again that I must never under any circumstances touch the brass knob. Only they were to handle it! However, the way it glowed and reflected the flames was so dazzling that it presented a huge temptation. I couldn't imagine why my grandparents were so unkind as to keep to themselves the wonderful things that would evidently follow from touching it.

So it was that, on one occasion when they had slipped momentarily out of the room, I moved the fireguard and grabbed hold of the knob. I ended up in the accident and emergency unit!

Some of us learn the hard way the consequences of disobedience!

116

Archbishop Thomas à Becket, in T S Eliot's play **Murder in the Cathedral**, *realising that he is on a moral course that will lead him to martyrdom, fends off three tempters who try to persuade him to do the wrong thing. But then:*
The fourth temptation is the greatest treason;
To do the right thing for the wrong reason.

117

BBC Radio 4's *Medicine Now* reported recently on scleroderma, a condition in which the skin and other soft tissues gradually thicken and harden. The sufferer is unable to move joints; the lungs thicken and hamper breathing; the heart tissue may thicken and heartbeats become infrequent. Those who suffer from the physical disease do so through no fault of their own.

Not so with the spiritual equivalent, which the Bible calls 'hardening of the heart'. It begins with becoming thick-skinned...

118

The Telegraph, April 1997:
Steve Balsamo, who stars in the London production of *Jesus Christ Superstar*, has been given a lighter cross to bear. He will now carry a 28 lb crucifix, rather than the 170 lb version that was threatening to damage his spine.

119

Martin Niemoller, Lutheran pastor, imprisoned for preaching against Nazism:
In Germany, the Nazis came for the Communists, and I didn't speak up because I was not a Communist. Then they came for the Jews, and I didn't speak up because I was not a Jew. Then they came for the trade unionists, and I didn't speak up because I was not a trade unionist. Then they came for the Catholics and I was a Protestant, so I didn't speak up. Then they came for me ... By that time there was no one left to speak up for anyone.

120

How much opposition could you take and still stand firm? As much as Jean Moulin faced as he motivated the resistance movement to oppose Nazism during the Second World War?

Arrested in 1943, he was tortured by Klaus Barbie in Lyons. He was brutally beaten for many days. When he could no longer hear but could just see, the Nazis, still trying to discover his real identity, held in front of him a paper on which was written: *'Etes vous Jean Moulins?'* Moulin took a pencil and crossed out the 's'.

It was his one admission. He knew everything; he said nothing.

121

When Jesus rose from the dead, the stone was rolled back by an unknown hand, and the wax seal that had been placed upon it by Pilate's guards was broken. To interfere with the seal of the Roman governor was a serious crime. This means that whatever other all-surpassing significance the resurrection had, its first significance was as an act of civil disobedience.

122

On 30 July 1996, four young Christian women from Liverpool appeared in court charged with criminal damage for completely disarming a British Aerospace Hawk – with household hammers! Their defence was 'lawful excuse', because the plane was destined to be used by the Indonesian government to bomb civilians in East Timor which it has illegally occupied since 1975, during which time one third of the population has been murdered.

To the surprise of many (including themselves) the women were acquitted.

123

William Reel, writing in The Times:
In highbrow circles, ridiculing Jews is Nazism, ridiculing blacks is racism, ridiculing feminists is sexism, but ridiculing Christians is freedom of speech.

124

On 20 October 1968 Ethiopian Mamo Wolde won the Olympic marathon. Over an hour later Tanzanian John Akhwari finished last, leg bleeding after a serious fall. A reporter asked him, 'Why did you bother to carry on with a serious injury and no hope of coming anything but last?'

He panted, 'My country did not send me seven thousand miles to Mexico to start a race. They sent me seven thousand miles to finish it.'

125

In the remote hills of India, the missionary doctor was about to close up his clinic. It had been a long day and he was tired. It was only out of pity that he stopped himself locking the door when he saw a man limping in terrible pain toward the entrance. 'I've walked twenty kilometres from my mountain village because they said you would help.' Sighing, he let the man in and showed him to a chair.

The doctor looked down at the man's bare feet. They were ruined with disease – swollen and covered with sores. He worked on them for nearly an hour, rubbing in ointment and bandaging them. 'Your feet will be well again now,' he said kindly. 'However, there is something you must do.' He went to a shelf at the back of the clinic and fetched a box. 'I am going to give you a pair of shoes. You must always, always wear them, and then your feet will be protected.'

The man's eyes lit up. When he tried on the shoes he could barely contain his gratitude.

Some months later the doctor took a mobile clinic to the villages remote in the mountains. You can imagine his delight when, as he entered one village, he saw the man whose feet he had treated. He was about to greet him as an old friend when, to his dismay, he saw the man hobbling toward him painfully on bare feet, swollen and covered with sores. The doctor almost wept: 'But where are your shoes?'

The old man smiled and beckoned. 'Come inside.' He led the doctor to his home. From under his bed he took a hand-somely carved, wooden box and opened it. There inside, wrapped in cotton, were the shoes. 'These shoes are my most treasured possession in the world,' he said proudly. 'They are so special that I wear them without fail... every Sunday.'

126

William Carey, nineteenth-century founder of the Baptist Missionary Society:
Attempt great things for God; expect great things from God.

127

G K Chesterton, twentieth-century novelist:
The Christian ideal has not been tried and found wanting. It has been found difficult; and left untried!

128

J R R Tolkien, writing in **The Hobbit**:
'Goodbye!' said Gandalf to Thorin.

'And goodbye to you all, goodbye! Straight through the forest is your way now. Don't stray off the track! If you do, it is a thousand to one you will never find it again and never get out of Mirkwood, and then I don't suppose I or anyone else will ever see you again.'

'Do we really have to go through?' groaned the hobbit.

'Yes, you do!' said the wizard. 'If you want to get out the other side. You must go through or give up your quest. And I am not going to allow you to back out now, Mr Baggins. I am ashamed of you for thinking of it.'

129

In Don Marquis' poem, **The Lesson of the Moth**, *Archy the cockroach tries to convince a moth that its determination to 'break into an electric light and fry himself on the wires' is futile. The moth argues:*
'It is better to be part of beauty for one instant, and then cease to exist, than to exist forever and never be part of beauty!'

The cockroach lamented, 'I wish there was something I wanted as badly as he wanted to fry himself'!

130

Adrian Plass, writing in **The Sacred Diary of Adrian Plass, aged 37 and a half**:
Some Christians seem to make people feel miserable and guilty, and they regularly check that their victims don't backslide into happiness.

131

John Woolmer, writing in **The Silent Voice**:
My mother used to tell the story of the country signalman who was found with one level crossing gate open and the other closed. When asked why, he said, 'I was half expecting

a train.'

If we only half expect God to act we may obstruct his coming.

132

Peter Graystone:
Beside my bed is a toy lamb, although you would barely recognise it as such. I have had it since the day I was born and its name is Larry. It is tattered beyond recognition. It used to be covered in white fluff, with a felt daisy in its mouth, but every last wisp of wool has fallen out and I ate the daisy.

However, it is my most treasured possession, forming an unbroken link back through every stage of my life. It has become a potent symbol. You see, it has reached such a pitiful state because it has been loved so much.

I offer it as a symbol to those for whom love has meant unrelenting years of disappointment, unrequited emotion, or unthanked sacrifice. It is these people who begin to understand the cost of the love of Jesus – and with that understanding comes his blessing.

133

*Margery Williams, **The Velveteen Rabbit**, Heinemann:*
'What is Real?' asked the Rabbit one day, when they were lying side by side near the nursery fender, before Nana came to tidy the room. 'Does it mean having things that buzz inside you and a stick-out handle?'

'Real isn't how you are made,' said the Skin Horse. 'It's a thing that happens to you. When a child loves you for a long, long time, not just to play with, but really loves you, then you become Real.'

'Does it hurt?' asked the Rabbit.

'Sometimes,' said the Skin Horse, for he was always truthful. 'When you are Real you don't mind being hurt.'

'Does it happen all at once, like being wound up,' he asked, 'or bit by bit?'

'It doesn't happen all at once,' said the Skin Horse. 'You become. It takes a long time. That's why it doesn't often happen to people who break easily, or have sharp edges, or who have to be carefully kept. Generally, by the time you are Real, most of your hair has been loved off, and your eyes drop out, and you get loose in the joints and very shabby. But these things don't matter at all, because once you are Real you can't be ugly, except to people who don't understand.'

134

Catherine Bramwell Booth:
The wild rose can only be a wild rose, a thistle can only be a thistle; to people only God gave the power to change their ways.

135

Long after his first retirement George Foreman, who had been heavyweight champion of the world in the 1970s, returned to the ring. In the intervening years he had become a Christian. He was asked what difference his new-found faith made to his attitude to the sport. He said, 'I can't bring myself to hate the other guy in the ring any more.'

Two years later he once again became world champion – the oldest in boxing history.

136

General Norman Schwarzkopf, Allied Chief of Staff in the 1991 Gulf War, mischievously hijacking the Bible:
A very great man once said you should love your enemies and that's not a bad piece of advice. We can love 'em but, by God, that doesn't mean we're not going to fight 'em.

137

Two men were sitting in a park, watching the world go by. The interest of one of them was taken by a middle-aged man sitting on a bench some distance from them. 'I'm sure that's our new bishop,' he said.

The other man looked across. 'It never is! He's too young to be a bishop.'

'I'm sure it is! I saw his photo in the newspaper. I'll bet you ten pounds it is.'

'You're on!' said his friend. 'How are we going to find out?'

'I'll go and ask him,' said the man confidently, and he walked over. 'Excuse me, but are you the new bishop of this diocese?'

The stranger grabbed him by the throat, squeezed so tight he could hardly breathe, and hissed at him, 'Look, pig-face, I'm having my lunch, and if you don't leave me alone I'm going to punch your teeth clean out of your mouth!'

The man regained his dignity as quickly as he could and returned to his friend. 'Well, what's the verdict,' he was asked.

'No good! The bet's off. He won't say whether he's the bishop or not.'

138

Sir Cliff Richard, singer:
Some impertinent young berk of a journalist ... asks me impertinent questions [and] I just want to clobber him on the jaw. But I don't, and afterwards I think, yes, that's the triumph really in my life, that I haven't hit as many people as I could have done.

139

Michael Ramsay, former Archbishop of Canterbury, had a deft way of dealing with the media. On his arrival in the USA he held a press conference. A journalist mischievously asked him, 'Archbishop, will you be visiting any nightclubs while you are in New York?'

With a innocent-looking twinkle in his eye, he replied, '*Are* there any nightclubs in New York?'

The danger of flirting with the media only emerged next day when his interview was reported under the headline:

'Archbishop's First Question On Arrival: Are There Any Nightclubs In New York?'

140
David Jenkins, former Bishop of Durham:
A bishop and a chief rabbi were in a boat on the Sea of Galilee when a wind blew up and the rabbi's skull cap was blown into the water. The bishop got out of the boat, walked across the water and collected the cap, returning it to its owner.

A reporter with a powerful camera lens was on the shore. The following day the headline in the newspaper read: 'Bishop Can't Swim.'

141
Festo Kivengere, Bishop of Uganda:
I'm just an ordinary Christian. There are no extraordinary Christians anywhere; just ordinary ones saved by an extraordinary Saviour.

142
Festo Kivengere tells the story of an incident with his wife Mera. They had been having a domestic 'difference of opinion'. He was due to speak at an evangelistic gathering in Kabale.

As he was about to leave, with the argument unresolved, he was convinced that the Lord was telling him to go and settle things with Mera. To Festo it felt as if he was arguing with the Lord, saying that there was no time – he had to go to the rally.

Then it was as if God said to Festo, 'OK, Festo! You go to the meeting if you must. But you are going alone. I'm staying here in the kitchen with Mera!'

Festo came to his senses, resolved the argument with Mera, and you can be absolutely sure that God was with him at the meeting!

143

Desmond Tutu, former Archbishop of Johannesburg:
My father used to say, 'Don't raise your voice; improve your argument. Good sense does not lie with the loudest shouters.'

144

David Sheppard, when he became Bishop of Liverpool, was asked what he was going to do with his new authority and power:
Listen and learn.

145

Experience is not what happens to you; it's what you do with what happens to you. Consider the example of Mrs Betty Tudor from Exeter. At the last count she had clocked up 273 hours of driving lessons. In that time she has exhausted nine instructors, and has been banned from three driving schools. She has only taken the driving test seven times, but has failed them all. On the last occasion she went the wrong way round a roundabout, and the examiner was so terrified that he insisted on driving the vehicle back to the test centre himself.

Some Christians go to their grave in ripe old age with their L-plates still attached. God longs for us to mature!

146

Letter written by an unknown hand to Diognetus in the second century:
You can't tell a Christian from a non-Christian by where he lives or the way he speaks or how he dresses. There are no 'Christian towns', there is no 'Christian language', and they eat, drink and sleep just like everybody else.

Christians aren't particularly clever or ingenious, and they haven't mastered some complicated formula like the followers of some religions. But while it's true that they live in cities next to other people, and follow the same pattern of life as they do, in fact they have a unique citizenship of their own. They are, of course, citizens of their own lands – loyal ones, too. But yet they feel like visitors. Every foreign country is their homeland, and their homeland is like a foreign country to them.

147

Lord Melbourne (when, in the late eighteenth century, William Wilberforce was denouncing the wickedness and injustice of the slave trade):
Things have come to a pretty pass when religion is allowed to invade public life.

148

George Austin, Archdeacon of York:
For the Christian, to mix religion and politics is not an option – it is an obligation.

149

St Teresa of Avila, sixteenth-century Spanish nun:
Christ has no body now on earth but yours, no hands but yours, no feet but yours. Yours are the eyes through which is to look out Christ's compassion for the world; yours are the feet with which he is to go about doing good; yours are the hands with which he is to bless men now.

150

Martin Luther, sixteenth-century German monk and leader of the Protestant Reformation, was asked what he would do if he knew that Christ was returning tomorrow. He replied:
Plant a tree today.

151

God wants spiritual fruit – not religious nuts!

152

*A A Milne, writing in **When We Were Very Young**:*
James James Morrison Morrison Wetherby George Dupree
Took great care of his mother, although he was only three.

James James said to his mother, 'Mother,' he said, said he,
'You must never go down to the end of the town unless you
go down with me!'

   *Good advice for the Christian's relationship with God as
well!*

153

George V was a strict disciplinarian with his sons. The
princes, you will remember, grew up to be Edward VIII, who
abdicated and became the Duke of Windsor, and George VI.
The Duke recalled that every day without fail, his father
would say to him, 'Never forget who you are.'

   As Christians living in a world with many different
approaches to life and morality, similar advice would be useful to us: 'Never forget *whose* you are.'

And finally...

154

Peter Graystone:
The challenge is for all the dozers to perk up, and all the
deserters to join up, and all the idlers to hurry up, and all the
loungers to sit up, and all the miseries to cheer up, and all the
bores to shut up, and all the whisperers to speak up, and,
most of all, for all the sleepers to wake up – because while
the disciples were sleeping, Jesus was betrayed.

Chapter 4

The way of the world

155

Peter Graystone:
I went to see a play at the Wyndhams Theatre in London. I looked at my ticket and made my way to seat D16, but as I edged along the row I realised there was someone in my seat. I hate it when that happens! I was just saying, 'Excuse m...,' when I looked down and saw who it was – Alan Rickman. Beside him were Frances Barber, Peter Brook and Jeanne Moreau. Alan Rickman realised what had happened and got out their tickets – sure enough they had D16 – D19.

I backed away murmuring, 'They'll find me somewhere,' but he said, 'No! We're here as guests of the theatre. The rule is, if you pay for the seat, you get it.' So they all got up and trooped off. I've no idea where they ended up!

There were three empty seats next to me throughout the whole play. I thoroughly enjoyed it, and at the interval I was thinking to myself that to get to these prime seats, I had shifted the leading actresses of both England and France, a Hollywood superstar, and a living legend!

On the way home on the train I looked at my ticket again, because I was using it as a bookmark. It wasn't D16; it was O16.

156

What they said about mistakes:
Abraham Lincoln, nineteenth-century president of the US: The man who is incapable of making a mistake is

incapable of anything.

Tallulah Bankhead, legendary Hollywood actress: The only thing I regret about my past is the length of it. If I had to live my life again I'd make all the same mistakes – only sooner.

George Santayana, Spanish philosopher: Those who refuse to learn from their own history are condemned to repeat it again and again.

An American newspaper, quoted in a letter by the painter Edward Burne-Jones: Correction of mistake: Instead of being arrested, as we stated, for kicking his wife down a flight of stairs and hurling a lighted kerosene lamp after her, the Rev James P Wellman died unmarried four years ago.

157
The Guardian, October 1995:
Publishers of *Easy Sky Diving* have hurriedly recalled all copies of the book to insert an erratum slip. It reads: Please make the following correction. On page 8, line 7, 'State zip code' should read 'Pull rip cord'.

158
A traveller, between flights at an airport, bought a packet of biscuits and sat down to read a newspaper. She heard a rustling sound and, from behind her paper, saw a neatly-dressed man helping himself to her biscuits. Not wanting to make a scene, she leaned over and took a biscuit herself. As he ate more, she grew angrier. She reached across to the packet more pointedly, and munched increasingly noisily.

Before long the biscuits were gone and the woman, now inwardly fuming, stood up to leave when her flight was announced. As she opened her handbag to get her ticket, she found her pack of biscuits, unopened!

159

Gene Brown, North American humorist:
If there were any justice in the world, people would occasionally be permitted to fly over pigeons.

160

What they said about work:

Bruce Grocott, writer: I have long been of the opinion that if work were such a splendid thing the rich would have kept more of it for themselves.

Campbell Christie, General Secretary of the Scottish Trades Union Congress: It is one of the contradictions of our society that two-thirds of people are stressed due to overwork, while one third are stressed due to under-employment and poverty.

Unnamed British MP, reacting to a pay rise which took his or her salary to £34,085: Our pay is pathetic.

Slogan of a 1970s advertising campaign: A housewife is not a toy.

Retired pilot of Concorde: When I was at fifty thousand feet, I sometimes used to wonder what was keeping me up there. I decided it was my monthly salary cheque.

Bertrand Russell, twentieth-century philosopher: Work is of two kinds. The first involves altering the position of matter relative to the earth's surface; the other consists of telling other people to do so. One is disagreeable and badly paid; the other is agreeable and well paid.

C Northcote Parkinson, English humorist ('Parkinson's law'): Work expands so as to fill the time available for its completion.

Roy McCloughry, writer and lecturer: A system of work which declares that what you are is what you are worth in the market place is fundamentally contrary to the kingdom of God. Where is there a place in economics for love?

161

Anita Roddick, founder of the Body Shop cosmetic retail chain:
I am still looking for the modern day equivalents of those Quakers who ran successful businesses, made money because they offered honest products and treated their people decently, worked hard, spent honestly, saved honestly, gave honest value for money, put more back than they took out, and told no lies. This business creed, sadly, seems long forgotten.

162

A specialist is someone who learns more and more about less and less until he knows everything about nothing. A generalist is someone who learns less and less about more and more until he knows nothing about anything.

163

From the situations vacant column of the BBC in-house magazine **Ariel**, *August 1992:*
Vacancy for a human resources assessment technologist corporate management development.

164

Dorothy Parker, writing in **The Little Hours:**
I'm never going to be famous. My name will never be writ large on the roster of Those Who Do Things. I don't do anything. Not one single thing! I used to bite my nails, but I don't even do that any more.

165

P G Wodehouse, twentieth-century novelist:
I spent the afternoon musing on life. If you come to think of it, what a queer thing life is! So unlike anything else.

166

Sidney Harris, twentieth-century North American journalist:

When I hear someone sigh, 'Life is hard,' I am always tempted to ask, 'Compared with what?'

167

The Big Issue, September 1997:
In Germany, delegates have come together for the first International Liars' Congress, held over three days in Berlin. The congress was the brain-child of life-long liar Helmut Stank, 45, who wanted to provide a forum for those who simply cannot tell the truth. From the outset, however, the project ran into problems.

'I sent out two thousand invitations,' explained Mr Stank, 'but most of the people didn't believe them, so we only had twelve acceptances, of which four were hoaxes.' The eight delegates who did attend found they had nowhere to stay, because Mr Stank had lied about finding accommodation for them. A Greek delegate left after the first day claiming his mother had died, which turned out to be completely untrue. A lecture by Helmut Kohl, meanwhile, turned out to be a damp squib, when the latter was revealed to be a meat-packer from Hamburg, rather than the German Chancellor.

'The whole thing was a huge success,' lied Mr Stank – whose real name is Werner Schmidt.

168

T S Eliot, twentieth-century poet:
Mankind can only stand so much reality.

169

The Times once asked for articles from its readers on the subject of 'What's wrong with the world?' One reply was very brief:
Dear Sir,
I am.
Sincerely yours, G K Chesterton.

170

The Times, December 1996:

In 1952 London endured a catastrophic attack of smog, which was so caustic that it killed twelve thousand people. It was impossible to see from one side of the road to another. And cinemas were closed because it was impossible to project the image as far as the screen ... But smog is not a thing of the past; it has simply become invisible. Londoners are still choking from the air they breathe, but unlike soot, the killer chemicals are impossible to see.

In a spiritual sense, as well as a physical one!

171

Eugene Ionesco, twentieth-century Romanian playwright:

The supreme trick of mass insanity is that it persuades you that the only abnormal person is the one who refuses to join in the madness of others; the one who tries vainly to resist.

172

The writer Malcolm Muggeridge used to speak of the decline of morality as if it were like frogs in a pan of water. If you put them in boiling water they jump out. But if you put them in cold water and heat it degree by degree, they stay to die.

173

Mae West, in the film **Klondike Annie***:*

Between two evils, I always choose the one I haven't tried before!

174

In the United Kingdom, what can you do and when?:

At 10 years: You can be tried in court.

At 13 years: You can work part-time.

At 14 years: You can consume soft drinks in a pub; draw money from a National Savings Account.

At 15 years: You can be sent to a youth detention centre; see a 15-certificate film.

At 16 years: You can marry with your parents' agreement; consent to sexual relations; claim social security benefits; drive a moped; leave school; buy fireworks; buy cigarettes and tobacco; choose your own doctor; leave home with your parent's consent.

At 17 years: You can be sent to prison; drive a car or motorbike; become a street trader.

At 18 years: You can vote; marry or emigrate without your parent's consent; buy and drink alcohol; give blood; be asked to sit on a jury; buy, sell, or mortgage a house; see 18-certificate films; be tattooed; change your name; gamble in a turf accountant; donate organs for transplant.

At 21 years: You can become an MP or local councillor; drive a bus or lorry.

175

What they said about power:

Adlai Stevenson, who ran against Dwight Eisenhower in the US presidential election of 1952, parodying Lord Acton: Power corrupts, but lack of power corrupts absolutely.

Kenneth Patchen, social commentator: God must have loved the People in Power, for he made them so very much like their own image of him.

Jon Wynne-Tyson, critic: The wrong sort of people are always in power because they would not be in power if they were not the wrong sort of people.

*Alexander Solzhenitsyn, writing in **The First Circle***: You only have power over people so long as you don't take everything away from them. But when you've robbed a man of everything, he's no longer in your power – he's free again.

*Aldous Huxley, writing in **Ends and Means***: So long as men worship the Caesars and Napoleons, Caesars and Napoleons will duly arise and make them miserable.

*Tom Stoppard, writing in **Squaring the Circle***: If you were handed power on a plate you'd be left fighting over the plate.

176

Peter Graystone:

Some teachers have more authority than others. A teacher was showing two new infants around his school, stressing how important it was for them to do precisely what the staff told them. Suddenly he saw an older pupil racing at full tilt along the corridor and shouted out his name reprimandingly, 'NEIL!' The two infants immediately knelt down!

177

The university's zoology exam was about to begin. As the invigilator strode to the front of the examination room there was tension among every student. 'This is an exam about the identification of birds,' he announced. And one student silently let out a whoop of delight. He had spent the whole of his revision time memorising pictures of birds and was confident of one hundred per cent success! The examiner explained that they would be shown slides and were to write down the name of each bird as it appeared.

The student smiled smugly as the lights went down and the first image appeared. It showed a bird's pair of feet. A slight disappointment came over him. He knew birds from their overall appearance, not just their feet! His hopes of one hundred per cent had gone. Never mind! Plenty more to come! The next slide came up. It showed another pair of feet. So did the next one. And so did the next one!

It was too much! 'Professor!' The examiner was as surprised as anyone else at this interruption. 'The examination is supposed to be about identifying birds. So far you have only showed birds' feet.'

'That is correct,' the examiner said patiently. 'The whole examination requires you to identify birds from their feet.'

The student panicked. 'But that's not fair. I've learnt to recognise birds from their overall size, shape and appearance.'

'Then you have learnt wrongly!' The student was furious. He leapt from his chair and made for the exit. The examiner went on, 'Young man, if you leave now you will fail the exam completely.'

'I don't care,' he snapped. 'If you can't make it fair now I've got no patience to wait.'

'You are the rudest student I have ever come across,' insisted the examiner. 'What is your name?'

And as the man stormed towards the door he paused for a moment, pulled his trousers up to his knees and shouted, 'Guess!'

178

Leaders talking about leadership:

Charles, Prince of Wales: A feeling of not knowing quite where we are is fairly widespread in human societies today. *(He was, in fact, in Australia!)*

David Mellor, broadcaster and former Member of Parliament: A national leader is only ever one sound-bite away from destruction.

John Major, former prime minister: By all means listen to a politician when he tells you what he plans. But ask him too: 'How will you do it?' Take it from me, the very devil can be in the detail.

Emperor Hirohito of Japan: You cannot imagine the extra work I used to have when I was a god.

179

Tony Blair, former lead singer of Ugly Rumours (oh yes, and he is also...):
I got fed up with all the sex and sleaze and backhanders of rock-and-roll, so I went into politics instead!

180

Albert Einstein, twentieth-century German physicist, originator of the theory of relativity:
The release of atom power has changed everything except our way of thinking ... If I had known I would have become a watchmaker.

181

Aldous Huxley, twentieth-century novelist:
Science has explained nothing. The more we know, the more fantastic the world becomes... and the profounder the surrounding darkness.

182

Noel Coward, twentieth-century playwright:
I have no more faith in men of science being fallible than I have in men of God being infallible, principally on account of them being men!

183

In April 1997, Professor Ian Plimer, Head of Earth Sciences at Melbourne University, Australia, successfully sued a creationist who claimed to have found Noah's Ark on Mount Ararat for engaging in 'conduct which is misleading or deceptive within the meanings of the Trade Practices Act.'

184

Why Engineers Don't Write Recipe Books, intercepted on the Internet:
Ingredients: 532.35 cm^3 gluten, 4.9 cm^3 NaHCO$_3$, 4.9 cm^3 refined halite, 236.6 cm^3 partially hydrogenated tallow triglyceride, 177.45 cm^3 crystalline C$_{12}$H$_{22}$O$_{11}$, 177.45 cm^3 unrefined C$_{12}$H$_{22}$O$_{11}$, 4.9 cm^3 methyl ether of proto-catechuic aldehyde, two calcium carbonate-encapsulated avian albumen-coated proteins, 473.2 cm^3 theobroma cacao, 236.6 cm^3 de-encapsulated legume meats (sieve size 10).

Instructions: To a 2-L jacketed round reactor vessel, with an overall heat transfer coefficient of about 100 Btu/F-ft^2-her, add the ingredients with constant agitation until the mixture is homogenous. Place the mixture piecemeal on a 300 x 600 mm sheet. Heat in a 460K oven for a period of time that is in agreement with Frank & Johnston's first order rate expression, or until golden brown. Once the reaction is complete, place the sheet on a 250 °C heat-transfer table, allowing the product to come to equilibrium.

Result: Chocolate chip cookies.

185

In the 1995 Hollywood feature film *The Net*, Sandra Bullock's character finds one day that her identity has been completely wiped off all computerised records and replaced with someone else's identity. She suddenly has a criminal record on police files and everyone assumes that she lives at another address. The real her has been deleted.

The film assumes that we live in a world in which anything from ordering pizza to retrieving records from halfway across the planet can be achieved through the vast, complicated map of phone lines and computers known as the Internet – a world in which, with the right knowledge and criminal intentions, a hacker could log into remote computers and alter any information he or she chooses.

No wonder people feel ill at ease!

186

After years of research and development, scientists are at last able to announce that they have invented a device which can infallibly detect even the minutest quantity of any kind of drug in the air about a person. It's called a parent.

187

Thomas Edison, the world-changing scientist and inventor, tried over two thousand materials in the search for one out of which could be manufactured a filament for the light bulb.

His assistant lamented, 'It is all in vain – we have learned nothing'.

Edison replied, 'That is nonsense. We have come a long way. We now know two thousand elements we cannot use to make a light bulb'.

188

Michael Faraday, famed for his pioneering work on electro-magnetism, was visited in his laboratory by the prime minister of the day. Gladstone was absolutely fascinated by the marvel of electricity. He had, however, a question: 'What possible practical use for it could there be?'

Faraday replied, 'Practical use, sir? Well, one day you will be able to tax it.'

189

Garrison Keillor, writing in **Lake Wobegone Days***:*
Santa Claus was not prominent in the pastor's theology. He had a gift of making you feel you'd better go home and give all the presents to the poor and spend Christmas with a bowl of soup, and not too many noodles in it either. He preached the gospel straight, and as he said, the gospel is meant to comfort the afflicted and afflict the comfortable. He certainly afflicted the Lutherans.

190

The *Independent* newspaper carried out a survey of 402 children of all kinds just before Christmas 1995, asking them what their biggest wish was for the world. By far the largest number replied: 'For everyone to be happy.' Close behind it were, 'Fighting and war to stop,' 'Everyone to have enough food,' and, 'No more accidents or disasters'. One boy suggested: 'For people to give your balls back when they land in their garden'.

191

Katharine Whitehorn, the **Observer***, December 1994:*
The confusions of the season reached their zenith last week, in my view, when a chorus of adoring school children on television were asked by their teacher, 'Now, who is the most important person at Christmas?' When they carolled, 'Father Christmas!' she said approvingly, 'That's right.'

So much for baby Jesus and all that stuff!

192

P J O'Rourke, writing in **Parliament of Whores***:*
Santa Claus is preferable to God in every way but one: there is no such thing as Santa Claus.

193

What puts the X in Xmas?:
Expenditure, expectation, excitement, excuses, excess, exhaustion, exuberance, exhibitionism, extravagance... and, if things go wrong, explosive expletives!

194

The XYZ of Christmas:
X-mas: An alternative name for Christmas devised by people who don't like it much and are determined to make it sound like a skin disease.
Y-mas: An obscure name for Christmas heard from behind the bathroom door as the cook tries to defrost the turkey under a hot tap minutes before the guests arrive: 'Why, why why?'
Z-mas: A dozy name for Christmas heard from the armchair as over-indulged relatives sleep off the space between the Queen's speech and the big film: 'Zzzzz!'

195

And so may I wish you the best possible Christmas, forgiven and at peace – with all your past forgotten, and all your presents remembered!

And finally...

196

What's the difference between *(the name of a male member of the congregation)* and a hot dog?
    (Name) wears boxer shorts, but a hot dog just pants!

Chapter 5

Death and beyond

197

Famous last words:

Lord Palmerston, British Prime Minister in the nineteenth century: Die, my dear doctor, that is the last thing I shall do.

Oscar Wilde, nineteenth-century writer: Either that wallpaper goes or I do.

Vespasian Caesar, fifty years after the ascension of Jesus: O dear, I think I am becoming a god.

Joseph Addison, eighteenth-century politician and writer: See in what peace a Christian can die.

O Henry, nineteenth-century writer: Turn up the lights; I don't want to go home in the dark.

John Wesley, eighteenth-century evangelist: The best of it is, God is with us.

Lytton Strachey, twentieth-century biographer: If this is dying, then I don't think much of it.

Emily Dickinson, nineteenth-century North American poet: The fog is rising.

Gertrude Stein, the North American writer, as her lover Alice B Toklas sobbed, 'What's the answer, what's the answer?': 'Well, what's the question?'

198

What the film director Woody Allen has to say about death: I don't want to achieve immortality through my work... I want to achieve it through not dying.

The difference between sex and death is that with death you can do it alone and no one is going to make fun of you.

Dying is one of the few things that can be done just as easily lying down.

Eternal nothingness is OK, if you're dressed for it.

There will be no major solution to the suffering of mankind until we reach some understanding of who we are, what the purpose of creation was, what happens after death. Until these questions are resolved we are caught.

199

Advertisement for an North American life insurance company in the early 1960s:
Death is nature's way of telling you to slow down.

200

James Thurber, North American humorist:
Early to rise and early to bed,
Makes a man healthy and wealthy and dead.

201

W C Fields, in the 1934 film You're Telling Me:
It's a funny old world – a man's lucky if he gets out of it alive.

202

George Bernard Shaw, twentieth-century playwright:
The statistics about death are very impressive. One out of every one dies!

203

The Guardian, May 1997:
A man arrested for running down the street naked in Melbourne, Australia, has been released. The police dropped charges against him when they discovered that he was running away from the mortuary where he had just mistakenly been pronounced dead.

204

When *Pepsi Cola* was launched in China, its marketing managers wondered why its famous slogan, 'Come alive with *Pepsi*,' was not achieving the impact that it had achieved elsewhere in the world. It was discovered that the translator had rendered it: '*Pepsi* brings your relatives back from the dead.'

205

The Archbishop of Canterbury, George Carey, is not unfamiliar with seeing things he says to reporters being given an unhelpful twist by their new context in newspapers. While he was Bishop of Bath and Wells, he commented on a decision to turn part of Shepton Mallet cemetery into a children's recreation area. The *Bristol Evening Post* reported him as saying, 'Graveyards too often have a morbid atmosphere because people associate them with death.'

206

From the Highway Code:
Do not enter the box unless your exit is clear.

207

Peter Graystone:
As a boy scout I learned how to lay a trail for others to follow. I wasn't the world's most enthusiastic scout, and on the list of things that didn't grip me, laying a trail is near the top! The sign I used most was a circle with a dot in the middle – either in stones or scratched into the forest pathway. It was supposed to mean 'gone home.' It actually meant that I had got fed up and didn't want to play any more!

It took on a whole new meaning when I saw the tomb of Lord Baden Powell, the founder of the Scout movement. On it is a circle with a dot in the middle – Gone Home.

208

President Charles de Gaulle describing himself:
Old man, exhausted by ordeal, detached from human deeds,

feeling the approach of the eternal cold, but always watching in the shadows for the gleam of hope.

209

Sue Rodriguez, a Canadian woman who loved skiing, was diagnosed in August 1991 as having Lou Gehrig's disease, which brings progressive paralysis while the mind stays active. She campaigned for four years on television and in court to have medically assisted suicides legalised – she maintained that denying them contravened the Charter of Rights. Her argument was always, 'Whose body is this? Who owns my life?' She became a familiar public figure as she took her case to the Court of British Columbia (unsuccessfully) and then to appeal (unsuccessfully). As the country watched, she looked progressively frailer. In September 1993 she went to the Canadian supreme Court, which ruled against her by five judges to four.

In the last days of her life, aged 43, she could not move, had to be spoon-fed, and every breath was a challenge. In January 1994 she told her husband Harry and her MP, Svend Robinson, that she had chosen to die on 12 February. She had dinner with her husband and nine-year-old son and they stayed until morning. An hour later the MP, who was a close friend, arrived with a doctor. The doctor administered a lethal injection, and Robinson held her in his arms for the rest of the morning. When she died peacefully, he called her palliative care doctor and the police. Tearfully, he later told a press conference, 'She was so strong and courageous right up to the point she began to lose consciousness. She told me to relax at one point'.

After her death, the Canadian parliament were prompted to debate euthanasia. The Right to Die Society of Canada backed it, but opponents (among them many Christians) allege that the organisation manipulated a vulnerable woman for political ends.

When asked how she wanted to be remembered, Sue Rodriguez replied, 'I want my son to be proud of me.'

210

Dame Cicely Saunders, pioneer in palliative care and founder of the hospice movement:
I have had much correspondence with the former chairman of the Euthanasia Society ... and I took him round Saint Christopher's [hospice for those who are terminally ill]. He came away saying, 'I didn't know you could do it. If all patients died something like this we could disband the society.' If you relieve a person's pain and if you make him feel like a wanted person, then you are not going to be asked about euthanasia.

211

The final entry in the diary of Captain Robert Scott on his attempt to be the first person to reach the South Pole, 1912:
We are pegging out in a very comfortless spot. Hoping this letter may be found and sent to you. I write you a word of farewell. I want you to think well of me and my end... Goodbye – I am not at all afraid of the end, but sad to miss many a simple pleasure which I had planned for the future in our long marches. We are in a desperate state – feet frozen etc, no fuel, and a long way from food, but it would do your heart good to be in our tent, to hear our songs and our cheery conversation... We are very near the end. We did intend to finish ourselves when things proved like this, but we have decided to die naturally without.

212

Charles Kingsley, nineteenth-century novelist:
It is not darkness that you are going to, for God is light. It is not lonely, for Christ is with you. It is not unknown country, for Christ is already there.

213

Last night I dreamed I went to heaven. The angel at the gate looked through his list and shook his head: 'I'm sorry, but it says here that you are not allowed to come in. There is a punishment for you – you have to go back and live your life again – with a ghastly, quarrelsome, ugly woman (*or man*).'

As I was bemoaning my fate, I suddenly caught sight of ... (*the name of a much-liked, unmarried male [or female] in the congregation*). He was walking along with a gorgeous beauty of a girl.

'It's not fair,' I protested to the angel. 'I know he's a splendid and good man, but he's not that much better than me.'

'No, you've got it all wrong,' said the angel. 'He's the punishment for the beautiful girl!'

214

An angel was giving a recent arrival a guided tour of heaven. Hectare after hectare of magnificently landscaped garden stretched as far as the eye could see. Thronging the lawns, lost in wonder and delight, were Methodists, Catholics, Orthodox, Anglicans, Salvation Army, Baptists (*make your own localised selection of denominations*). The newcomer and his guide passed through them, thrilled with the beauty of it all. They came to a huge, rose-covered wall. From behind it came the happy sound of feasting and rejoicing.
'What's going on in there?' asked the man.
'Shh!' The angel motioned to him to tiptoe past. 'It's a private garden. For the evangelicals (*substitute your own tradition*)! We don't like to spoil their party. They think they're the only ones here!'

215

Saint Augustine of Hippo, fourth-century African bishop:
We shall rest and we shall see; we shall see and we shall love; we shall love and we shall pray, in the end that has no end.

216

A mother writes:
The week my five-year-old's goldfish died was a bad week for the theme of the church service to be 'the living waters of

eternal life.' The confusion would not have mattered had we not gone for a walk past the local cemetery that afternoon. I explained that Grandma was buried here and had gone to heaven.

'You said my goldfish had gone there,' my son pointed out.

'That's right!'

There was a silence. 'I do hope Grandma can swim.'

217

Jacob Epstein's fabulous sculpture of Lazarus in the chapel of New College, Oxford, shows him from the rear, as if from inside the tomb, looking back over his shoulder with unbearable sadness at the Paradise he was leaving behind in order to retake his place on earth.

218

*Andrew Mosby, **Time Out** columnist:*

I became cynical about religion at the age of ten when I went into the gift shop of Westminster Abbey, asked for the gift of eternal life, and was laughed at. But I'm willing to forgive and forget!

219

A BBC researcher, preparing two satirical programmes, faxed their Catholic consultant asking how she could get the official Roman Catholic view on Heaven and Hell.

The answer which came back was brief but accurate: 'Die!'

220

*C S Lewis, writing in **Mere Christianity**:*

There are only two kinds of people in the end: those who say to God, 'Thy will be done,' and those to whom God says, in the end, 'Thy will be done.'

221
C S Lewis:
In hell, they talk a lot about love. In heaven, they just do it.
Hell is an unending church service without God. Heaven is
God without a church service!

222
Sonya, giving the closing words of Anton Chekov's play
Uncle Vanya:
All we can do is live. We'll live through a long row of days.
And through the endless evenings. And we'll bear up under
the trials fate has sent to us. We will constantly toil for oth-
ers, now and for the rest of our days.

And when we come to die, we'll die submissively. Beyond
the grave we'll testify that we have suffered; that we have
wept and known bitterness. God will pity us, you and I, dear
uncle. God will take pity on us.

And we, uncle, shall live a life of radiant beauty and
grace, and look back on this life of unhappiness with tender-
ness, and smile. And in that new life we shall rest, uncle. I
know it. I have faith. I have a passionate faith. We shall rest
to the songs of the angels in a firmament arrayed with jew-
els, and look down and see evil, all the evil in the world, and
all our own sufferings, bathed in a perfect mercy, and our life
grown sweet as a caress. I have faith...

You have had no joy in your life, I know. I know. But
wait and only wait, Uncle Vanya. We shall rest. We shall rest.
We shall rest.

223
Joseph Heller's magnificent comic novel, **Catch 22,** *is set on
a US Air Force station in Italy during the Second World War.
The hero Yossarian watches his friends fall victim to the
fighting one by one in bleakly farcical ways. They include
Lieutenant Dunbar, who was 'determined to live for ever or
die in the attempt'. The first time we meet him:*
He was lying motionless on his back again with his eyes

staring up at the ceiling like a doll's. He was working hard on increasing his lifespan. He did it by cultivating boredom. Dunbar was working so hard at increasing his lifespan that Yossarian thought he was dead ... How the hell else are you ever going to slow time down?

224

David Watson, the evangelist, on the eve of his tragically early death in 1984:
The church is the only society on earth that never loses a member through death! As a Christian I believe not just in life after death, but in life through death.

225

Sarah Miles, the actress, at the funeral of her husband Robert Bolt:
Until we come to terms with death and the dying process, we will always be driven by fear rather than love.

226

*Susan Sarandon, the actress who won the 1996 Oscar for her performance as Sister Helen Prejean in **Dead Man Walking**, a film about the death penalty, interviewed in the **Observer**:*
At my most vulnerable, what I fear most is leaving the children before I know they are happy and I know they are safe. But actually, it's good to have to think about death. Death's what's real in life. It's just that we find ways to be busy. If we lived every day with death, we would live a different life and it would not necessarily be a depressing one. It would probably be more joyful.

You know, I often lose the ability to prioritise. I'm rushing to get lunch for the children, and put the toilet paper on the toilet paper thing, and read the scripts, and it takes a kid getting sick or something to remember that it's not so important that there's stuff all over the floor and maybe, just maybe, you should play with your kids. People say that if we think about death all the time we'd go mad, but maybe we'd go sane.

227

Henry Scott Holland, nineteenth-century preacher:
Death is nothing at all... I have only slipped away into the next room. I am I and you are you. Whatever we were to each other, that we are still. Call me by my old familiar name, speak to me in the easy way which you always used. Put no difference in your tone; wear no forced air of solemnity or sorrow. Laugh as we always laughed at the little jokes we enjoyed together. Play, smile, think of me, pray for me. Let my name be ever the household word that it always was. Let it be spoken without effort, without the ghost of a shadow on it. Life means all that it ever meant. It is the same as it ever was; there is absolute unbroken continuity. Why should I be out of mind because I am out of sight? I am waiting for you for an interval, somewhere very near, just around the corner. All is well.

228

Jim Elliot, martyred missionary to the Auca people, 1956:
When it comes to die, make sure all you have to do is die.

229

Dorothy Parker, the North American humorist, suggested this epitaph for herself:
Excuse my dust.

And finally...

230

On a mercilessly sweltering summer evening, a New York priest took the opportunity to preach the shortest (and theologically most dubious) sermon in history. His opening – and closing – words from the pulpit were:
'You think this is hot? Be good!'

Chapter 6

Church and worship

231

Seeing a man about to fling himself off a tower block, his neighbour ran toward him shouting, 'Stop! Don't kill yourself. Give me a chance to offer you a message of hope!'

'What is there to live for?' muttered the suicidal man.

'Don't you believe in God?'

'Yes I do!'

'What a coincidence – so do I! Are you Jewish or Christian?'

'Christian.'

'What a coincidence – so am I! Protestant or Catholic?'

'Protestant.'

'What a coincidence – so am I! Anglican or non-conformist?'

'Anglican.'

'What a coincidence – so am I! Evangelical or liberal?'

'Evangelical.'

'What a coincidence – so am I! Charismatic or conservative?'

'Charismatic.'

'What a coincidence – so am I!' Spirit-baptised or Spirit-filled?'

'Spirit-baptised.'

At this, the man looked aghast, turned purple with outrage and yelling, 'Die, heretic!', he pushed him over the edge.

232

Connor Cruise O'Brien, politician and journalist:
Nothing does more to activate Christian divisions than talk about Christian unity.

233

*Leader of the **Independent** newspaper:*
All rows about religion in Britain now have a surreal quality. So few people know what the argument is about – or care.

234

The minister knew that the quality of the worship would improve if the piano were moved from one side of the church to the other. So he put the change he proposed to the committee. There was a furious debate about it. The meeting divided into two immovable camps – one for the move and one against any change whatever. The minister could not persuade the committee to reach unity... so he moved it one inch every week for three years!

235

Peter Graystone:
I had been invited to preach at a forward-looking church in Scotland. After a service full of joy, I was talking to members of the congregation over a cup of coffee. I asked one elderly gentleman how long he had been coming to the church. 'As long as I've lived in this town,' he said. 'And I've lived in this town for nearly sixty years.'

'Sixty years at one church!' I was impressed. 'I'll bet you've seen a lot of changes in that time.'

'I have,' he said proudly. 'And I've opposed every one of them!'

236

Dennis Lennon, writing about the history of the church:
External attacks merely produced a more fervent and loving church. So Satan put down his battering ram and tried germ warfare.

237

Anthony de Mello, Indian Jesuit:

When the guru sat down to worship each evening, the ashram cat would get in the way and distract the worshippers. So he ordered that the cat be tied up during evening worship. After the guru died, the cat continued to be tied during evening worship. And when the cat expired, another cat was brought to the ashram so that it could be duly tied up during evening worship. Centuries later, learned treatises were being written by the guru's scholarly disciples on the liturgical significance of tying up a cat as part of worship.

238

Peter Graystone:

My all-time favourite television advert was for the public service sector union *Unison*. So popular was it with my friends that we asked the press office to send us a list of all 130 spot times so that we could gather round the set, glass in hand, and join in with it!

It is a black and white animated cartoon. A lumbering, but lovely, white bear is sitting in the path. From the left of the screen an ant scampers in carrying a leaf. In a tiny high-pitched squeak he says, 'Excuse me! Excuse me!' The bear looks puzzled, but doesn't register. So the ant goes away and comes back with another. They both squeal 'Excuse me! Excuse me!' The bear tilts his head to one side, but the message is definitely not getting through. So the ant goes away again and comes back with ten thousand of his mates. They all rear up on their back legs and the noise is deafening: 'Get out the way!' The bear scarpers. The ants go their way. And a voice reassuringly tells us, '*Unison* – because there are some things you cannot do by yourself.'

It was only watching it for the twentieth time that I realised why I belonged to a church. But when I described the advert from the pulpit one Sunday and heard a packed congregation yell back, 'Get out the way!' I knew I wasn't the only one who made the connection!

239

President Franklin Roosevelt was a member of a Washington church, but was frequently away from his congregation on official business. One day the telephone rang in the rector's office and an eager voice asked, 'Do you expect the President to be in church this Sunday?'

'That,' said the rector, summoning up patience, 'I cannot say. However, we expect the Lord Jesus Christ to be there, and we fancy that will be incentive enough for a reasonably large attendance.'

240

A down-and-out was sitting on the step of a suburban church and weeping. To his astonishment, Jesus came walking along the street, and sat down beside him. 'Why are you crying?' Jesus asked.

'They won't let me in,' he said.

'I know how you feel,' sighed Jesus, 'I haven't been able to get in there myself for years.'

241

Peter Graystone:
Dear Mrs Helderly,

I am writing to invite you to Funkhouse Nightclub next Saturday night. This letter is part of a special effort to attract over 70s. We have been concerned because the number of people in that age range who attend has dropped dramatically.

We would ask you, though, not to wear your sensible shoes because they are not appropriate for a building where serious dancing takes place. One or two of our customers are concerned that your perm might cause offence to the young, so we would be obliged if you could consider dying your hair a more suitable vivid colour, or having it spiked. We would ask you also to leave your walking stick and bus pass outside since these are distracting to those trying to concentrate on the music. Hoping to see you there... in the distance.

Yours sincerely, Una Xeptable.

PS Thank you for your invitation to church last Sunday. I'm sorry not to have come, but I can't see myself fitting in.

242

There is nothing easy about being a new leader. At the farewell service of a retiring minister, an elderly lady said to him, 'The person who takes your place will not be as good as you.'

'I'm sure that won't be so,' replied the minister, secretly delighted.

'Take my word for it,' sighed the lady. 'I've lived through six ministers at this church and each one has been worse than the last.'

243

The Guardian, October 1995:
Only in America could a Methodist minister have received a glowing citation from the Sales Executive Club as the 'Most Sales-minded Clergyman'. He told the salesmen to pray, 'Lord, fill me with enthusiasm for my product.'

244

The Independent, October 1995:
Kellie Everts, who calls herself an ordained minister and a 'stripper for God' because she delivers sermons while performing, is filing a $40 million lawsuit against Morton Downey Jr, because she was outraged at her treatment on his extraordinary television show.

245

Why are ordained people described as priested? If a woman becomes a doctor has she been doctored? If she is training to be a cook, will she be cooked?

246

Groucho Marx, the legendary comedian, was thanked by a

clergyman for all the enjoyment he'd given to the world. He replied:
And I'd like to thank you for all the enjoyment you've taken out of it.

247

Isn't it remarkable what surgery can do for you these days! My friend has got such a bad memory that he went to see a consultant about the possibility of having a brain transplant. You can't get an operation like that on the National Health Service, of course, so one of his first questions was, 'How much is it going to cost?'

'Well sir,' enthused the surgeon as she showed him round, 'that all depends on what kind of brain you want to have transplanted. Here, for instance, is a professor's brain. That comes at one hundred pounds per gramme.' She moved along the shelf of brains, perfectly preserved in medical jars. 'And here is a Nobel prize-winning brain. That costs two hundred pounds per gramme.' With a flourish, she took down a jar which she obviously treasured. 'And here – here is a vicar's brain.'

'Now that sounds just what I want,' said my friend. 'How much is that?'

'A vicar's brain costs ten thousand pounds per gramme.'

'Ten thousand pounds! Why is it so much more expensive than the others?'

'Oh sir!' The surgeon shook her head. 'Have you any idea how difficult it is to get an ounce of vicar's brain?'

248

Apparently *(the name of the leader of your church)* has been away on a conference this week. He has been meeting with the leaders of other religions to help understand and respect each other.

Although the conference itself was a great success, the centre in which they were staying was fraught with problems.

It emerged on the first night that the manager had over-booked, and that there were not enough rooms. Wringing his hands with regret, he asked whether anyone would be pre-pared to spend the night in a barn outside the main building. A Muslim leader graciously agreed to, and left to find out what he had let himself in for.

Minutes later he returned and explained that, although he was more than willing to sacrifice his comfort, there was a pig in the barn. Because of his religion, he could not in good faith spend the night in close proximity to a pig.

This turned out not to be a problem, because a Hindu leader immediately agreed to take his place. The others breathed a sigh of relief, but it was not long before he returned. He had not realised that there was also a cow in the barn and, profusely apologetic though he was, it was not appropriate for someone of his faith to keep company with a cow.

This is where *(name)* showed his true character. Insisting that he did not mind in the slightest, he decided to forego his comfortable bed and headed for the barn.

Two minutes later there was a knock on the door of the conference centre. It was the pig and the cow.

249

W H Auden, twentieth-century poet:
A preacher is a person who talks in someone else's sleep.

250

*Andrew Brown, **Church Times**, March 1997:*
It is difficult to get platitudes heard. This must be the justifica-tion for the behaviour of the very wonderful Rev Earlsley White [of Uddington, Central Scotland], who arranged for his sermon on the dangers facing missionaries to be interrupted by a man with a gun...

The intruder, whose face was painted, held a hand gun to the minister's head and told 250 cubs and guides, their parents and leaders, that religion had caused a lot of trouble in the world. Most of the adults realised that the incident had been staged when the man talked about missionaries being persecuted for their beliefs. But some of the younger children started to cry as [the minister] was tied up and led out of the church. The congregation then heard two shots being fired.

The Sunday afternoon service, to commemorate the founders of the Scout movement, was stopped by the police a short time later after a member of the public reported seeing a gunman enter the church. Armed police sealed off the street outside the building and a police helicopter hovered overhead as the 69-year-old minister was interviewed. Mr White told officers from Strathclyde Police that he was trying to illustrate the theme of the sermon. He was later charged with obstructing the police and [his friend was charged] with firearms offences.

251

Sydney Smith, nineteenth-century writer, deploring the roguish behaviour of a friend in a letter to Lady Holland:
He deserves to be preached to death by wild curates.

252

Henry Hawkins, a nineteenth-century diarist, writing about an assize sermon:
It was a divine sermon. It was like the peace of God – in that it passed all understanding. And like God's mercy – it seemed to endure for ever.

253

Robert Warren, **Being Human Being Church***, Marshall Pickering:*
I wonder whether God desires, at the end of each sermon, to be able to hold up the life of ... the preacher and say, in true *Blue Peter* style, 'And here is one I prepared earlier.'

254

Former Archbishop of Canterbury Robert Runcie was about to preach in Japan when he read on the badly translated

order of service:
The Archbishop will give a massage.

255
A clergyman was delighted to be invited to take part in a big Christian convention. He spent hours preparing, gathering all his best material from years of preaching, all his best jokes and illustrations, in order to give a knock-out talk. When he got to the platform he discovered, to his dismay, that he had misunderstood the invitation. He wasn't supposed to speak; only open in prayer. Determined to make an impression, he managed to pray for fifteen minutes, incorporating most of the material into his prayer.

He began, 'Lord God, to help you understand the humility with which we come before you to pray, may we illustrate it with an anecdote.'

256
The curate had stepped in to take the service at very short notice because the vicar was ill. At the end of the sermon he explained apologetically, 'At such short notice I'm afraid I just had to rely on the Holy Spirit. Next week I hope to do better!'

257
It is frightening what one little misprint can do. A Baptist church in West London advertising a celebration service accidentally printed on the flyer:
The service will be Spirit-led. It will be gin with prayer.
I wonder how the spirit influenced that service. Hic!

258
Hildegard of Bingen, twelfth-century abbess and composer:
Be not lax in celebrating. Be not lazy in the festive service of God. Be ablaze with enthusiasm. Let us be an alive, burning offering before the altar of God.

259

Gerald Kennedy, writer:
That the gospel is to be opposed is inevitable; that the gospel is to be disbelieved is to be expected; but that it should be made dull is intolerable!

260

*In a rare interview (in the **Independent**), the singer Morrissey was asked how he would like to be perceived by his public:*
As always he took time to consider his reply. 'I'm not being funny,' he said eventually, 'but I'd settle for a blind adoration.' Tonight ... the fans will invade the stage, embrace their hero, dance, sweat, sing along and weep. In short they will adore him, blindly.
   True worship?

261

Several healing miracles took place at the Church of St Medard in Paris in 1732. There was such excitement that services there were in danger of getting out of hand. Emperor Louis XV had the gate of the church locked and a sign placed on it: 'By order of the king, God is hereby forbidden to work miracles in this place.'

262

Church of England Newspaper, November 1990:
A San Antonio priest went to amazing lengths to muffle the piercing wails of tone deaf former choir member Eulogia Maoias, who insisted on singing along at anthem time. Father Anthony Wrangler took out an injunction. When she ignored that, the police were called and she was taken into custody.

263

Boy George, singer:
The church badly needs a facelift, because it is God's theatre on earth, and he should be packing them in.

264

The BBC was not allowed to broadcast the wedding service of the future King George VI and Lady Elizabeth Bowes-Lyon (the Queen Mother) in 1923 because the Dean and Chapter of Westminster Abbey objected, stating that 'men may be listening in public houses with their hats on.'

265

Forty years ago, in a church in Yorkshire, a stained glass window of great beauty was being dedicated to God. 'What's it for?' whispered a small girl.

Her father replied. 'It's in memory of all the men and women who died in the services.'

There was an anxious pause, before the little girl asked, 'Did they die in the morning services or the evening services?'

266

Church Times, May 1997:
At Peterborough Cathedral, the ceremonies of the new light on Easter Sunday morning were being performed with great dignity and solemnity. Adrienne Davidson of Stamford in Lincolnshire tells us that, as the Bishop lit the Paschal candle, her two-year-old started singing: 'Happy birthday to you!'

267

The ideal text to hang on the wall of a crèche for the children of the church is 1 Corinthians 15:51:
We shall not sleep, but we shall be changed.

268

New Directions in Children's Ministry, the 1995 London Bible College consultation (with apologies to Rudyard Kipling!):
If you're excluded from the family meal,
If you speak and no one listens, but you cry and everyone 'tuts',
If you're sad but no one asks you what's the matter,

If you don't have a vote because your opinion's not valued,
If you can't read and you're expected to; or if you can and
you're not given a book,
If you have faith, and no one believes you,
If you come bearing gifts and no one accepts them,
If you're not getting value for money,
If you try your best for a right answer and only get a laugh,
If you bring your worship and everyone thinks it's entertainment,
    Then you are a child.
If you think the aisle is for cartwheels,
If you can laugh at the preacher but not at his jokes,
If you say, 'God is wicked' and know it's OK!
If you don't give a toss about getting wet,
If you enjoy writing on walls,
If just by your presence you bring others joy,
If you're prepared to take risks and ask questions,
If you're the role model for the kingdom,
    Then you are a child.

269
*Children in the Way, the report on all-age worship of the
Church of England General Synod Board of Education,
(Church House Publishing):*
Imagine a group of people of all ages going on a long walk
together. At times the children and adults will walk along
together, talking as they go, sharing stories with first one person and then another, each observing different things and
sharing their discoveries. At times the children lag behind
and the adults will have to wait for them and urge them on.
Sometimes the smallest children will ask to be carried. At
other times, though, the children will dash ahead making
new discoveries and may, perhaps, pull the adults along to
see what they have found. Some adults may well behave like
these children, of course. For all there will be times of
progress and times of rest and refreshment, time to admire
the view and times of plodding on, and the eventual satisfac-

tion of arriving at their destination.

Of course, a pilgrimage is something more than a hike. Traditionally it is a group of people of all kinds of ages united in reaching a common goal. They stop at significant places on the way. They exchange their own stories, and share past experiences and memories of those who have gone before them. They look forward to the rest of the journey, and to reaching their ultimate destination.

270

What they said about prayer:

John Wesley, eighteenth-century evangelist and founder of Methodism: Today I have such a busy day before me that I cannot possibly get through it with less than two hours' prayer.

Karl Barth, twentieth-century theologian: To clasp hands in prayer is the beginning of an uprising against the disorder of the world.

St Teresa of Avila, sixteenth-century Spanish Carmelite nun: From silly devotions and sour-faced saints, good Lord deliver us.

Mother Teresa of Calcutta, nun and founder of the Missionaries of Charity: We need to find God and he cannot be found in noise and restlessness. God is the friend of silence... the more we receive in silent prayer, the more we can give in our active life.

Orson Welles, film director and actor: I don't pray. I don't want to bore God.

Abraham Lincoln, nineteenth-century president of the US: I have been driven many times to my knees by the overwhelming conviction that I had nowhere else to go. My own wisdom and that of all about me seemed insufficient for the day.

William Temple, twentieth-century Archbishop of Canterbury: When I stopped praying, coincidences stopped happening!'

271

Michael Caine, actor:

My father was a Catholic and my mother Protestant. I was educated in a Jewish school, and my wife is a Muslim. I've watched the way they all ill-treated each other, so I rather feel outside of all that. But I certainly believe in God. It's just God and me, watching all the rest. I don't usually say prayers; I say thank you. If you'd had my life you'd spend more time saying thank you than asking for things.'

272

Phyllis Diller, North American comedienne:

You really want God to answer your prayers? A 62-year-old friend of mine went to bed at night and prayed, 'Please God, give me a skin like a teenager's.' Next morning she woke up with pimples.

273

G K Chesterton, twentieth-century novelist:

You say grace before meals. All right, but I say grace before the concert and the opera, and grace before the play and pantomime, and grace before I open a book, and grace before sketching, swimming, fencing, boxing, walking, playing, dancing, and grace before I dip the pen in ink.

274

Tom Davies, broadcaster, who found on a pilgrimage across England that 'the English remain a faithful people, fond of the practice of prayer and trusting in God's future good plans for us':

In a sense the country is one vast, secret web of prayer and, if the Son of Man were to return tomorrow, huge sections of the country would be prepared and ready.

275

Stephen Gaukroger and Nick Mercer, writing in **Frogs in Cream:**

A mother overheard her young son praying one day: '... and if you give me a bike, then I'll be good for a whole week.'

She interrupted him and said, 'Now Johnny, it's no good trying to bargain with God. He won't answer prayers like that!'

A few days later she overheard him praying again: '... and if you give me a new bike, Lord, I'll be good for *three* weeks!'

'Johnny,' said his mother gently, 'I thought I told you it was no good trying to strike bargains with the Lord. He doesn't respond to that kind of prayer.'

A few days later she was cleaning out the house and, to her amazement, found right at the bottom of the airing cupboard, a little statue of the madonna that had stood on the sideboard. She guessed this must be something to do with Johnny and went up to his room to find him. He wasn't there but on the window sill she found a note which read: 'OK Lord, if you ever wont to see yor muther again...'

276

James and Harry always enjoyed staying overnight with their grandparents. Before bedtime they sat together on the bed for prayers. Ten-year-old James prayed, 'Lord God, please look after Mummy and keep us all safe tonight.'

Then his seven-year-old brother bellowed at the top of his voice, 'Dear God, please let me get a Bart Simpson T-shirt for my birthday.'

'You don't have to shout,' said James. 'God isn't deaf.'

'No,' whispered Harry. 'But Grandad is!'

277

Nine-year-old James still has a lot to learn about prayer. After a test at school today he realised that he had left it too late to do the working and praying that should have been done last week. So tonight he prayed, 'Lord God, please make Sydney the capital of New Zealand!'

278

The minister had been invited to Sunday lunch by a family in the congregation. Dad asked him to say grace, but the minister replied, 'Why don't we let your young son Jackie say grace?'

Jack froze, 'I don't know what to say.'

'That's all right,' said Mum. 'Just say exactly what Daddy said to God at breakfast this morning.'

'Oh that's easy,' said the boy, shutting his eyes tight. 'O God, is it today that boring old man's coming to lunch?'

279

When his parents invited the minister for Sunday lunch after the service, four-year-old Douglas was watching carefully. The food was put on the table and the clergyman was invited to say grace, which he did. Douglas observed: 'You don't pray so long when you're hungry, do you?'

280

Chagford Parish News, September 1997:
There will be a pot-luck supper in Chagford Church Hall next Thursday, followed by prayer and medication.

281

A man went on a lion hunt. Suddenly a huge lion bounded toward him, fangs flashing. As the lion approached, the man lined up his gun, waited and... click! No bullets! In a terrified panic, the man dropped to his knees and began to pray. The lion hurtled toward him and, just as it reached its prey, went down on its knees as well.

'What are you doing?' stammered the terrified man.

The lion snarled, 'Saying grace!'

282

Stephen Pile, in The Book of Heroic Failures, nominates the worst save in footballing history:
This honour falls to Señor Isadore Irandir, goalkeeper of the

Brazilian team Rio Preto, who let in a goal after three seconds. From the kick off in the soccer match between Corinthians and Rio Preto at Bahia Stadium, the ball was passed to Roberto Rivelino who scored instantly with a left-foot drive from the halfway line. The ball went past the ear of Señor Irandir, while he was on his knees finishing pre-match prayers in the goalmouth.

283

Notice outside a church in Adelaide:
Why pray when you can worry and take tranquillisers?

284

... which at least is better than this notice outside a Leeds church:
Don't let worry kill you. The church can help.

285

Julian of Norwich, fourteenth-century writer and mystic:
Pray inwardly, even if you do not enjoy it. It does good, though you feel nothing, see nothing, yes, even though you think you are doing nothing. For when you are dry, empty, sick or weak, at such a time is your prayer most pleasing, though you find little enough to enjoy in it. This is true of all believing in prayer.

286

C S Lewis, twentieth-century writer and academic:
The moment you wake up each morning, all your wishes and hopes for the day rush at you like wild animals. And the first job each morning consists in shoving it all back; in listening to that other voice, taking that other point of view, letting that other larger, stronger, quieter life come flowing in.

287

In George Bernard Shaw's play *St Joan*, Joan of Arc frequently hears God speaking to her. The French king is annoyed and jealous that he doesn't share her experience. He cries out: 'O your voices, your voices, why don't your voices come to me?'

Joan replies: 'They do come, but you do not hear them. You have not sat in the field in the evening listening to them.'

288
Peter Graystone:
We live in a world that requires instant everything! Instant coffee, which saves you waiting for it to percolate. Instant money, from a machine in the wall that saves you having to queue inside the bank. Instant meals, heated at the press of a button without the bother of chopping a single vegetable.

What next? Perhaps the microwave heater, so that you can have a long, relaxing evening in front of the fire in eight minutes! And then the microwave prayer, which can be done during a commercial break of a TV programme, saving you a whole evening's effort of turning out for the church prayer meeting! Maybe microwave justice, which will peacefully resolve centuries-old conflicts at the press of a computer button, avoiding those dreadful arguments, conferences and battles!

History shows that patient prayer counts!

289
In 1863, Abraham Lincoln called a national day of prayer and fasting in North America. The president himself wrote the official proclamation announcing it:
We have been the recipients of the choicest bounties of heaven. We have been preserved these many years in peace and prosperity. We have grown in numbers, wealth and power as no other nation has ever grown. But we have forgotten God. We have vainly imagined, in the deceitfulness of our hearts, that all these blessings were produced by some superior wisdom and virtue of our own. Intoxicated with unbroken success, we have become too self-sufficient to feel the necessity of redeeming and preserving grace, too proud to pray to the God who made us.

290

Buzz Aldrin, second astronaut to set foot on the moon, writes of the events immediately after touch-down on the June afternoon in 1969:

I unstowed the elements in their flight packets. I put them and the scripture reading on the little table in front of the abort guidance-system computer. Then I called Houston: 'Houston, this is Eagle ... I would like to request a few moments' silence. I would like to invite each person listening in ... to contemplate for a few moments the events of the past few hours, and to give thanks in his own individual way.'

For me, this meant taking communion. In the blackout I opened the little plastic packages which contained bread and wine. I poured wine into the chalice my parish had given me. In the one-sixth gravity of the moon, the wine curled slowly and gracefully up the cup. It was interesting to think that the very first liquid ever to be poured on the moon, and the first food eaten there, were consecrated elements...

I sensed especially strongly my unity with our church back home, and with the church everywhere. I read, 'I am the vine; you are the branches. Whoever remains in me, and I in him, will bear much fruit; for you can do nothing without me.'

291

Justin Martyr, second-century writer and evangelist:

On that day which is called after the sun, all who are in town gather together for a communal celebration. Then the memoirs of the apostles are read for as long as time allows. When the reader has finished, the president speaks, exhorting us to live by these noble teachings. Then we all rise together and pray ...

When the prayer is finished, bread and wine are brought. The president gives thanks as well as he can, and all the people reply with the acclamation, 'Amen'. After this the [bread and wine] is distributed to everyone, and the deacons are sent to take them to those who are absent.

Those who are well-to-do make gifts, each just as he wishes. These gifts are collected and handed over to the president. He it is who assists the orphans and widows, those who are in want through sickness or for some other reason, prisoners, strangers passing through, all who are in need.

292

*A reporter from the **Independent** visited Albania after the fall of communism in that country:*
A young woman told me that during the years when religion was banned, this church was used as a school gym: 'If a girl was naughty or inattentive, she was punished by having to stay on afterwards to paint over the church murals ... I was born in 1967, the year they abolished religion, but I was secretly baptised at the age of two. My grandmother taught me the liturgy and on Easter Day she secretly painted some eggs red. That may sound childish, but to me it was very beautiful and wonderful ...'

Socialist art, with its strident, boastful exaltation of power, is empty, indeed repulsive. The architecture is uniformly depressing and hideous. Even the mass-produced clothes are coloured the drabbest of browns and greys. The Albanians have lived with no more spiritual, emotional or artistic nourishment than could be found in the speeches of Enver Hoxha, or art and literature of which he approved. Things which we take for granted, such as a fine mediaeval church, a hymn ... the words of Psalm 23, or even an egg painted red for a little girl's Easter present, seem to Albanians beautiful and wonderful.

293

*Carl Lawrence, writing about China in **Against All Odds**:*
In 1966 the Red Guards made a concentrated effort to burn all Bibles, hymnals and other Christian literature. Today it is not uncommon to see a group of several hundred people with only one Bible.

One lady had a complete Old and New Testament. She

would bring it to the meeting wrapped in linen. When the pastor read the scriptures, he would gently take the Bible, carefully unwrap it and read the text. After he was finished, he would return the Bible to the lady and she would wrap it up in the linen cloth as others had done to the Lord's physical body.

In some houses, certain people are told in advance what scripture will be needed for the next meeting. Each of them will copy one verse and bring it. When the leader wants to lead or speak from scripture, he collects the handwritten copies, puts them all together and he will have the text. In this way, if the police interrupt the meeting, the Bible will not be lost.

294

How much do you value the Bible? A comparison from Roman mythology:
The Sybil wrote books of prophecy which she tried to sell to King Tarquin of Rome. She offered him nine volumes for 300 gold pieces. When he declined them, she burnt three, then offered him six for the same price. He refused again. She burnt another three and offered him the three that remained at the original, full price. He bought them.

295

Irina Ratushinskaya, the poet, interviewed in the **Telegraph** *in December 1986 after being released from a Russian concentration camp:*
I was twenty-three before I ever saw a Bible. But I had already known God for many years and could talk to him. I found in the Bible what I had already discovered alone.

296

Brother Andrew, founder of Open Doors missionary society:
Too many people don't want the Bible to interfere with their Christianity.

297

David Richardson, lawyer and clergyman:

What do you give a Pharisee to eat when you invite him to dinner?

The starter would have to be kosher, of course, because of the rigorously strict food regulations that he has to follow, as in Mark 7:3: 'The Pharisees and all the Jews do not eat unless they give their hands a ceremonial washing.'

The main course would be whole camel, as in Matthew 23:24: 'Woe to you blind guides! You strain out a gnat but swallow a whole camel.'

For dessert I recommend widow's house pudding, as in Luke 20:47: 'They devour widows' houses and for a show make lengthy prayers. Such men will be punished most severely.'

298

The Hip Ten Commandments, from **The Black Bible Chronicles**, *a paraphrase aimed at black American street kids:*

1. Don't put anyone else before me.
2. Don't make any carved objects or things that look like what's in heaven or below – and don't bow down to these things like they're something heavy.
3. Don't dis the Almighty's name.
4. Give honour to mom and dad and you'll live a long time.
5. Don't waste nobody.
6. Don't mess around wit someone else's old man or old lady.
7. You shouldn't be takin' nuthin' from your homeboys.
8. Don't tell lies on your homebuddies.
9. Don't go round wanting to crash in a bro's home.
10. Don't want what you can't have – it ain't cool.

299

We marked the beginning of Lent with a Shrove Tuesday pancake party. It was in fancy dress. You had to go dressed as the thing you were giving up for Lent. I went wearing nothing!

300

Riding into the holy city of Jerusalem has long been regarded as a claim to greatness. In 1917, many centuries of Turkish rule came to an end when the British allies retook Jerusalem. On December 11 General Allenby, approaching Jerusalem, declared, 'Far be it from me to enter this holy city in the manner of he who is my king and only Saviour.' He dismounted his jeep and walked into Jerusalem.

301

Peter Graystone:
In some churches, Palm Sunday is marked by receiving a palm leaf, shaped as a cross. It is a meaningful and charming tradition, but does it capture the spirit of Jesus' entry into Jerusalem? Palms are only mentioned in one gospel account, but three of them mention the throwing of cloaks. Laying down one's cloak before a king for him to walk on was an ancient symbol of complete submission (as, for instance, in 2 Kings 9:13 at the accession of Jehu).

Suppose we developed a new custom on Palm Sunday – taking off our overcoats and throwing them into the aisles for our fellow Christians to walk over. Let's rename it 'Overcoat Sunday'. What a sign of submission that would be! It cost the witnesses to the entry into Jerusalem a great deal to throw down what would have been their only cloak for Jesus to walk on. Does our submission to Christ have the same totality? My guess is that Palm Sunday would become 'Second-best Overcoat Sunday' or 'Jumble Sale Overcoat Sunday'.

302

A boy threw a stone at a stained glass window. It nicked out the 'e' of the word 'highest' in the text 'Glory to God in the Highest'. Thus until it was mended, it read 'Glory to God in the High St'. Mending it only substituted one truth for another!

303

In a large church in Birmingham, there had been torrential rain overnight, which overflowed the drains and sent a mess of leaves floating in huge puddles. It was difficult even to get in the front door. The pastor of the church had asked three people who were regularly involved in cleaning the church to do some frantic sweeping in order to make it easier for people to enter. The result was that they were the last people to come into the service, well after it had started.

Standing at the front of the church, the pastor saw them coming in, and realised that there was nowhere left for them to sit. He whispered across to the guitarist who was leading the singing, 'Three chairs for the cleaning team.'

The musician completely misheard him, and shouted out, 'Hip hip!' And the congregation roared back, 'Hooray!'

304

In Sudan, the Muslim government has pushed displaced people far out into the mountains. The Christians are not allowed to build a permanent church (obviously it would be threatening to the government). Very early every Sunday morning, local men erect a scaffolding structure which allows some shade for everyone. It takes hours. Then after the service, it is all taken down again. What a picture of the dedication of God's people in another land to being servants of the church! And also of the fact that the church is not a structure; it is a people on the move.

305

In 1996, the International Olympic Committee commissioned a worldwide survey to investigate the world's best-recognised logos. For them, it uncovered good news. However, it gives Christians much to ponder:

Olympic games	92%
Shell	88%
McDonalds	88%
Mercedes	74%

Christian cross	54%
Red Cross or Red Crescent	47%
United Nations	36%
Football World Cup	36%
World Wide Fund for Nature	28%

306
D T Niles, writer:
Evangelism is no more than one beggar telling another where to find bread.

307
Philip Mohabir, considering his call as a missionary from Guyana to England, in **Building Bridges***:*
England? Missionary? Impossible! The Queen lives in England. People in England do not sin. It is a Christian country. They do not need missionaries; they send them!

308
Max Warren, former General Secretary of the Church Missionary Society:
Our first task in approaching another people, another culture, another religion, is to take off our shoes, for the place we are approaching is holy. Else we may find ourselves treading on men's dreams. More serious still, we may forget that God was here before our arrival.

309
David Sankster, a North American student, went from a lifetime in Manhattan to the Dominican Republic to serve as an agricultural missionary. He had no background in agriculture or any ability to speak Spanish, he just knew (his church leaders having confirmed his calling) that God had told him to go.

His first attempts at farming were lamentable. After about a fortnight the Spanish-speaking farmers took pity on him. After farming their own fields they would go over to help Dave, for which he was profoundly grateful. However, he possessed one skill that the local people lacked. He could read!

Some of the local farmers had been given books in Spanish on improved farming techniques. Each night Dave would read words in a language he did not understand, the farmers interpreted them and put into practice what they had learned. Within eighteen months their agricultural productivity was up by 300 per cent.

It was then that they began asking Dave why he had come to them.

310

There are times when our support of mission is so weak that it seems as though Jesus' last words were, 'Go out into all the world, keep your head down, and don't open your mouths if you can possibly help it!'

311

A schoolteacher with a class of five-year-olds suddenly felt faint and dropped to the floor. As she went down she called out, 'Go and get the caretaker.'

Lying on the floor she was dimly aware of a crowd of young faces looking down at her, and a tiny voice saying, 'Which one of us do you want to go?'

312

An old man on the seashore was slowly picking up some of the countless small sea creatures which had got stranded on the beach at high tide, and throwing them back into the ocean. A passing jogger laughed, 'Just look at the beach – there are thousands of them all dying on the sand! What difference will what you are doing make?'

The old man looked patiently at the handful of creatures he was about to release into new life in the water: 'I don't honestly know. But it will make all the difference in the world to these.'

313

Andrew Graystone, broadcaster:

Dear God,

I am writing to thank and praise you yet again for the extraordinary vision which you have made so clear to me in recent weeks. Your commission to take the good news to the community is still burning in my veins. As you suggested, I have discussed your call at our recent church meeting. Here are the results:

There are 158 members in our church, but 44 said they were either too old or too young for that sort of thing.

That leaves 113 to get involved, but 36 said they do enough for the church already.

That leaves 77 to get involved, but 42 said they don't like to make a fuss.

That leaves 35 to get involved, but 22 are sure someone else would do it better.

That leaves 14 to get involved, but 13 say they wouldn't know what to do.

So that leaves me.

Where do we start?

Your loving servant, Me.

And finally...

314

What's the connection between John the Baptist and Winnie the Pooh?

They have both got the same middle name.

Chapter 7

People and relationships

315

In the Lion Handbook of Christian Belief, George Carey writes of a sixth former who dazzled a debate with a persuasive speech arguing that the hope of civilization lies in the pursuit of scientific knowledge and that religion has no place. At the end of the year, he asked the headmaster for a college reference:

The man wrote: 'John is a living organism. Group: vertebrates. Class: mammalia. Order: primates. Genus: homo sapiens.

'Chemical description: a large quantity of carbon; some gallons of water; various amounts of iron, calcium, magnesium, mineral salts.

'Psychological description: a mind; intellectual, emotional and volitional powers; instincts. IQ 130.

'I hope that John will fit as an admirable unit into the various machines, industrial, commercial and so on, that make our scientifically-planned society. But regrettably I have serious misgivings about this. There is something in John that refuses to be 'cribbed, cabined and confined' and reaches out to a fulfilment beyond the capacity of a machine-like destiny to supply. In his eager pursuit of scientific knowledge and love of music, as well as in the discontent to which he once confessed at his inability to live up to ideals, it seems to me that John is on a quest that existence, even in a four-dimensional space/time continuum, can never satisfy.'

John asked for his reference to be rewritten. The

headmaster had left out of his account what it means to be human.

316

How much do you think you are worth? Not very much, according to a 1991 Readers' Digest analysis of an average human being. We are made up of the following:
Enough fat for seven bars of soap; enough iron for a medium-sized nail; enough sugar for seven cups of tea; enough lime to whitewash a chicken shed; enough phosphorus to put the tips on 2200 matches; enough magnesium for one dose of salts; enough potash to explode a toy crane; enough sulphur to rid a small dog of fleas.

But because we are in God's image...

317

BUPA medical insurance advertisement:
Your brain is the most complex structure known to man. Your eyes can distinguish up to 1 million colour surfaces. Your lungs are big enough to cover half a tennis court. You have around 60 thousand miles of blood vessels. Your skin is constantly replacing itself. You give birth to 100 billion red blood cells every day. Your bones are as strong as cast iron. Your heart beats 100 thousand times a day. You're amazing! We want you to stay that way.

318

Robert, 27, interviewed in **Cosmopolitan,** *after spending £8,000 to have silicon implants in his chest and legs:*
Arnold Schwarzenegger is my idol, and whether God intended me to be like him or not, that is what I have always wanted.

319

St Francis of Assisi, thirteenth-century Italian founder of the Franciscans:
What I am in God's sight is what I am. No more; no less!

320

A comment about Trevor Huddlestone, missionary and anti-apartheid campaigner, by a biographer:
What impresses his friends, including those who do not share his faith, is his insistence on assuming that they are better people than they really are; which makes them feel better, and probably be better.'

321

In Fynn's biography, **Mr God, this is Anna,** *a six-year-old girl reveals a simple and startling understanding of God and human nature:*
At the top corner of the street was a house that was a lot bigger than the rest. In this house lived Milly, Sally, Corey, and a few other young ladies ... Given other circumstances they would have been different, but with poor homes, little education, and even less money, prostitution was the only way they knew how to make money ...

Many times Anna and I have sat with them and so often the talk turned to the subject of religion and God. The passing years have made me realise that they were among the few people who could admit to themselves that they were sinners. What was puzzling for me was that some of the girls' customers regarded themselves as good, solid citizens... What puzzled Anna was how such nice people could be called 'dirty'.

Milly taught Anna how to make bead belts, necklaces and bracelets. All the adults for streets around knew what the girls did, but it was only Anna and her friends and me who knew what they could do.

322

Anna:
The difference from a person and an angel is easy: most of a angel is in the inside and most of a person is on the outside.'

323

Keith Boot, the **Independent on Sunday,** *July 1993:*

Love – the case for: A many-splendoured thing; a growing or full constant light (Donne); strong as death (Solomon); means never having to say you're sorry (Eric Segal, although the present author has spent hours of his life saying sorry to various beloveds); makes the world go round.

Love – the case against: A sickness full of woes (S Daniel); an abject intercourse between men and slaves (Goldsmith); just a four-letter word (B Dylan); a potential sin in theology; a forbidden intercourse in jurisprudence; a mechanical insult in medicine; a subject philosophy has no time for (Kraus, cheery old soul!); makes the world go round.

324

Basil Hume, Cardinal Archbishop of Westminster, declaring that 'homophobia should have no place among Christians':
To love one another, whether of the same sex or of a different sex, is to have entered the area of the richest human experience.

325

Oscar Levant to the composer George Gershwin:
Tell me, George, if you had to do it all over would you fall in love with yourself again?

326

*Yip Harburg, **Tennyson Anyone?**:*
In the spring a young man's fancy lightly turns to thoughts of love;
And in summer,
And in autumn,
And in winter –
See above!

327

What they said about marriage:
   Billy Connolly, comedian: Marriage is a wonderful invention; but then, so is a bicycle repair kit.

Mae West, film star: Marriage is a great institution, but I'm not ready for an institution yet.

Erica Jong, writing in **Fear of Flying***:* Bigamy is having one husband too many. Monogamy is the same.

Helen Rowland, North American writer: Marriage is like twirling a baton, turning handsprings, or using chopsticks: it looks easy till you try.

A P Herbert, twentieth-century humorist: Holy deadlock!

Or from the other point of view:

George Bernard Shaw, writing in **Man and Superman***:* Marriage is popular because it combines the maximum of temptation with the maximum of opportunity.

Martin Luther, sixteenth-century theologian: There is no more lovely, friendly or charming relationship, communion or company than a good marriage.

Ogden Nash, twentieth-century North American poet: Marriage is the only known example of the happy meeting of the immovable object and the irresistible force.

Rainer Maria Rilke, twentieth-century German poet: A good marriage is that in which each appoints the other guardian of his solitude.

328
William Tyndale, sixteenth-century father of the Bible in English:
Marriage was ordained for a remedy, and to increase the world, and for the man to help the woman and the woman the man, with all love and kindness.

329
In November 1988 a woman from Somerset spent £10,500 reconstructing her daughter's wedding in its entirety. The reason was that she didn't like the video of the actual event and wanted it filmed again.

330

Peter Graystone:

I was best man to a good friend, and he stayed at my flat overnight after the stag party so that we could go down to the church together. I took him an early-morning cup of tea while he was in the bath. 'Hey, I've just been thinking,' he laughed, 'this is my last bath as a virgin.'

That really tickled me, so after a superb service (as a wedding between two Christians so often is) and a formal reception, I decided during the evening disco to tell his new wife what he had said. She looked at him, standing there with sweat dripping down his shirt and the unmistakeable, wafting smell of over-energetic dancing in a small room, and she declared, 'That was not your last bath as a virgin!'

331

Yip Harburg writes of the perfect honeymoon in **Courtship in Greenwich Village***:*

Our days will be so ecstatic,
Our nights will be so exotic,
For I'm a neurotic erratic,
And you're an erratic erotic.

332

Temple Gairdner, twentieth-century missionary to the Middle East:

That I may come near to her, draw me nearer to thee than her. That I may know her, make me to know thee more than her. That I may love her with the perfect love of a perfectly whole heart, cause me to love thee more than her and most of all. Amen. Amen.

That nothing may be between me and her, be thou between us, every moment. That we may be constantly together, draw us into separate loneliness with thyself. And when we meet breast to breast, my God, let it be on thine own. Amen. Amen.

333

Warren Beatty, the actor, interviewed in **Vanity Fair** *about being married after a large number of casual affairs:*
Sex is great ... The highest level of sexual excitement is in a monogamous relationship.

334

Ronan Keating, lead singer of **Boyzone:**
I would like to think I will only sleep with the woman I marry. I will sleep with someone only when I'm ready to be a father, because that's what my religion says.

335

A Church of England General Synod Board of Education survey, 1992:
When asked how much they accepted of what their religion teaches about sex, 23% of 14 to 18-year-olds said nothing; 20% said not much; 18% said some; 9% said most of it; 6% said all of it. However, 24% did not know what the teaching of their religion was about sex.

336

The vicar was completely discouraged by the fact that his congregation looked bored and fidgety during his sermons. He wondered if he might as well stop bothering. 'Whatever am I going to do?' he wheezed to his wife. 'I might as well preach about taking the dog for a walk – they wouldn't even notice what I was talking about.'

'But you don't know anything about dogs!' replied his wife. 'It's me who goes round the park with Rover every day.' And that was the last he saw of her that weekend. He lovingly kissed her goodbye as she went off to look after her ailing mother for a couple of days.

In fact it was that kiss which put an idea into the vicar's head. He knew how he would startle the congregation into listening. He would preach about something urgently relevant, he would be outspoken, practical and honest – he would preach about sex! And he did. It was brilliant – funny, touching, moral, spiritual – everything a good sermon should be. In fact it was so helpful that one of the ladies felt she had to phone up his wife as soon as she got home. 'Your husband was marvellous,' she gushed. 'Such wise and carefully chosen words, and such a brilliant choice of subject.'

'Well, you amaze me,' said the wife. 'To be perfectly honest I thought he had chosen a disastrous subject. In fact, he's only done it twice. The first time he got bitten on the leg, and the second time he got breathless and had to come home.'

337

Malcolm Muggeridge, twentieth-century journalist:
Sex is the mysticism of materialism and the only possible religion in a materialistic society.

338

John Lydon, aka Johnny Rotten of the Sex Pistols:
Some people need cheap sex, instant selfish gratification. Fine! But it makes me more miserable than ever.

339

After the banns of marriage were read for a couple at St John's, Hebburn-on-Tyne, the vicar led the congregation in prayer for their wedding and marriage:
And we pray that they may have wisdom in the conduct of all their affairs.

340

Tamasin Day-Lewis, producer of a Channel 4 documentary series on adultery:
I haven't yet been able to find a happy adulterer.

341

In the seventeenth-century, Robert Barker and Martin Lucas, the king's printers, were taken to the Court of the Star Chamber by the Archbishop of Canterbury, William Laud, and fined £3,000. Their crime had been printing and publishing an edition of a thousand copies of the Bible in which a key word had mistakenly been omitted from one of the ten commandments. It was the seventh commandment – the one that forbids adultery. It was the word 'not' which was missing!

342

On page two of the Sun was a sobering news report:
Men who watch too many porn films are four times as likely to become impotent because they get bored by the images they see of the body, Italian sex expert Andrea Dotti warned yesterday.

Opposite this on page three was a photo of a naked woman, captioned:
Pud looking. Wendy is aged 19 and likes making desserts. But she never trifles with flans. So here's a nice pieful from the Dorset lass – served without topping.

Did no one on the editorial team notice the irony?

343

Intercepted on the Internet:
Last year my friend upgraded his GirlFriend 3.1 to GirlFriendPlus 1.0 (marketing name: Fiancee 1.0). Recently he upgraded Fiancee 1.0 to Wife 1.0 and it's a memory hogger – taken all his space.

Some features I'd like to see in the upcoming GirlFriend 4.0: A 'don't remind me again' button; shut-down feature; an install-shield feature so that GirlFriend 4.0 can be completely uninstalled if so desired (so that you don't lose cache and other objects).

I tried running GirlFriend 2.0 with GirlFriend 1.0 still installed. They tried using the same I/O port and conflicted. Another thing that sucks – all versions of GirlFriend that I've used are totally 'object orientated' and only support hardware with gold-plated contacts.

Virus warning: Wife 1.0 has an undocumented bug. If you try to install Mistress 1.1, Wife 1.0 will delete MSMoney files before doing the uninstall itself. Then Mistress 1.1 will refuse to install, claiming insufficient resources.

344

A sign outside a school in Berkshire reads 'St Margaret's School of the Immaculate Conception for Girls'. And the line underneath: 'Preparatory for Boys'.

345

Mike Barfield, an entry in A Dictionary for our Time:
To woo: See 'to wit'.

346

In August 1972, Soviet newspapers reported that a man called Darsan Yilmaz, who lived at Dalmali on the Black Sea, had been deeply disappointed at a rejection by his neighbour's attractive daughter. He decided he would abduct the girl by night.

He climbed a ladder, threw a blanket over her sleeping form, dashed to the car whispering romantic reassurances into her ear, and sped away. Safely outside the city, he ripped away the blanket to find not his girlfriend but her 91-year-old grandmother.

347

A woman had a teenage son who persistently had no interest whatever in Christianity. Every Sunday she would nag him, 'Won't you come to church with us?' And every day she would ask, 'Have you said your prayers today?' She put little tracts between his pillows when she changed the bed sheets, and Bible verses under his sandwiches when he took a packed lunch to school. It was all to no avail.

One day, in despair, she dropped to her knees and prayed fervently that whatever the obstacle was to her son becoming a Christian, God would take it away. There was a flash of lightning, and she completely disappeared!

348

In September 1990, Helmut Klein took his son Andreas to German high court. Why sue him? To make him clear up the records, light-bulbs, underwear, empty drink cans and dirty plates in his room.

349

Simon Gray, writing in **Otherwise Engaged***:*
'What have you got against children?'

'Well Steve, in the first place there isn't enough room. In the second place they seem to start by mucking up their parents' lives, and then go on in the third place to muck up their own. In the fourth place it doesn't seem right to bring them up into a world like this in the fifth place, and in the sixth place I don't like them very much in the first place. OK?'

350

Antoine de Saint-Exupery, writing in **The Little Prince***:*
Grown-ups never understand anything for themselves, and it is tiresome for children to be always and forever explaining things to them.

351

Sting, the musician, interviewed in **Rolling Stone***:*
When I was young my overwhelming ambition was to be famous. I wanted it so much so that my parents would be forced to notice me.

352

P J O'Rourke, writing in **All the Trouble in the World***:*
Are we disheartened by the break-up of the family? No one who ever met my family is!

353

There are three signs of growing old. The first is going grey, the second is losing your train of thought in mid sentence, and the third is... er...

354

In splendid old age, Winston Churchill was still sitting as a Member of Parliament. In the lobby of the House of Commons, he overheard a young MP whisper to another, 'They say the old man's getting a bit past it.'

As he blustered past he murmured to them, 'And they say the old man's getting a bit deaf as well.'

355

Basil Hume, Cardinal Archbishop of Westminster:
A society which treasures the elderly and disabled and looks after them is a generous society. Once this stops, life becomes cheap.

356

Brian Astbury, father of Siamese twins born in 1997:
Termination was mentioned, but for us it was never an option. Our babies will be born out of love into love.

357

T S Eliot, writing in Choruses from the Rock:
When the Stranger says, 'What is the meaning of this city?
Do you huddle close together because you love each other?'
What will you answer? 'We all dwell together
To make money from each other,' or, 'This is community'?

And finally ...

358

Margaret Thatcher, former Prime Minister, interviewed in Woman's Own, 1987:
There is no such thing as society. There are individual men and women and there are families.

Chapter 8

Money and possessions

359

What does £1 million buy?

40 heart transplants, 55 kidney transplants or 250 hip replacements;

2,702 kits to feed 810,810 Sudanese refugees;

565 full-time places in nursery education for one year;

71 new London constables;

5,555 meals at *Le Manoir aux Quat' Saisons* restaurant;

Two sponsorship deals between Nike and footballer Ian Wright;

143,061 copies of this book!

Reconciliation with God? Absolutely not! That is totally priceless – and absolutely free!

360

The China Daily, August 1993:

A farmer who buried his life savings in his backyard found that they had rotted away. Zhang Dexaing, a farmer of 82 who lives in the province of Liaoning, buried about £1,500 five years ago. He discovered that the money had been eaten away by mould and mildew when he went to dig it up.

361

What they said about wealth:

Colonel Sanders, founder of the vast multinational Kentucky Fried Chicken chain: There's no reason to be the richest man in the cemetery. You can't do any business there.

Spike Milligan, comedian: Money can't buy you friends – but you can get a better class of enemy.

Hugh Grant, actor: They love me in Japan. But unfortunately I don't want their love. I want their money.

Katherine Mansfield, twentieth-century writer: I must say I hate money, but it's the lack of it I hate most.

Madonna, singer: Do you really think I'm a material girl? I'm not. Take it! I don't need money; I need love.

Neil Simon, singer: Money brings some happiness, but after a certain point it just brings more money.

Michael Chang, tennis player: The money's great, but it won't last. The honour's great but it won't last. What will last is the love of Christ in my heart.

362

Richard Pryor, the North American comedian, was critically burned in an accident. Appearing later on the Johnny Carson Show, he insisted that when you are seriously ill, money isn't important:
All that I could think of was to call on God. I didn't call the Bank of America once.

363

*The **Independent**, December 1989:*
A Sikh businessman living in Vancouver said that a discovery in the Christian Bible had made him give away his £62 million fortune to the poor and start his working life over again. Stephen Sander, who made the money in property after arriving in Canada thirty years ago as a refugee from Pakistan, put his twenty-three apartment buildings into a trust to help the sick and hungry in the developing world – rents being used to finance aid projects. He said, 'I'm a poor man now. I want to be. I will have to earn my living the same way as anybody else. There's a saying about what good would it do if you were to acquire the world and lose your soul.'

364

George Gifford, A Discourse of the Subtill Practices of Devilles by Witches and Sorcerers, 1587:
For this is man's nature, that where he is persuaded that there is the power to bring prosperity and adversity, there he will worship.

365

Logan Pearson Smith, twentieth-century writer, writing in Afterthoughts:
Those who set out to serve both God and Mammon soon discover that there is no God.

366

Albert Schweitzer, doctor and missionary to Africa:
If there is something you own that you can't give away, you don't own it – it owns you.

367

Long ago when a king converted to Christianity and ordered his knights to be baptised, many of them held their right arms out of the water. As they were submerged in the waters, every part of them was baptised except the hand in which they held their weapon. When the crisis came, they could kill without having to feel constrained by Christian morality.

Is there an equivalent today? I sometimes wonder whether some Christians would prefer to hold their wallets and purses out of the waters of baptism. Certainly we act from time to time as if all of us belongs to God except what belongs to us!

368

In ancient legend, Saint Benedict, riding from chapel one Sunday, met a peasant. 'You've got an easy job,' said the peasant. 'Why don't I become a man of prayer, then I could ride on horseback?'

'What makes you think praying is easy?' responded the

monk. 'If you can say the Lord's Prayer just once without your attention wandering from the holy God, I'll give you the horse!'

The astonished peasant leapt at the opportunity. 'Our Father, who art in heaven, hallowed be thy name, thy kingdom come, thy...'. Suddenly he stopped and looked up at Benedict, 'Will you give me the saddle as well?'

369

General Charles Gordon, the nineteenth-century soldier whose service in Khartoum won him lasting fame, declined both a title and a financial reward from the British government. After some persuasion he accepted a gold medal inscribed with a record of his thirty-three military engagements, which became his most prized possession.

After his death it went missing. It was only later, when his diaries were unearthed, that it was discovered that, on hearing the news of a severe famine, he had sent the medal to be melted down and used to buy bread for the poor. He had written in his diary: 'The last earthly thing I had in this world that I valued I have given to the Lord Jesus Christ today.'

370

Jim Elliot, missionary martyred by the Auca tribe of Ecuador in 1956:
He is no fool who gives up what he cannot keep in order to gain what he can never lose.

371

St Augustine of Hippo, fourth-century African bishop:
God wants to give us something, but he cannot because our hands are full – there's nowhere for him to put it.

372

C S Lewis, writing in **Mere Christianity***:*
I do not believe one can settle how much we ought to give. I am afraid the only safe rule is to give more than we can spare.

373

Clive James, writing in **Unreliable Memoirs***:*

At the harvest festival in church the area behind the pulpit was piled high with tins of IXL fruit for the old-age pensioners. We had collected the tinned fruit from door to door. Most of it came from the old-age pensioners!

374

Once upon a time there was a prince who lived in a grand castle. Every day he would leave his castle in a splendid carriage to visit the daughter of the duchess in her palace. One day, by the beautiful gate of the castle, he noticed what looked like a tattered heap of rags squatting miserably. 'That poor beggar,' he thought to himself. He opened the window of the carriage and tossed a coin out so that it landed just at the foot of the bundle.

The next day he saw the dismal sight again. Once again he threw a coin from his window and hurried by. This grew into a habit each day, and the prince thought less and less about what he was doing. It didn't cost him much, after all!

Then one morning, he got held up by a particularly annoying courtier. He was in such a rush that he told the coach driver: 'Fast as you can! Go, go, go!' The driver lurched off at speed, cutting all the corners in the courtyard and scattering the servants. He sped through the gate so fast that the carriage was on two wheels and, splat, it crashed straight into the heap of rags and sent it flying ...

It was not a beggar; it was a crate of rotting bananas.

375

A pig and a hen were walking past a church. On the noticeboard, an accusing finger pointed at the passers-by, asking the question: 'What will you do for the poor?'

'I know what we could do,' clucked the hen to the pig. 'We could team up and lay on a bacon and egg supper to raise money!'

'It's all right for you to suggest that,' grumbled the pig. 'For you that would be a gift; for me it would be a sacrifice!'

376
Helder Camara, Archbishop of Recife, Brazil:
May your bounty teach me greatness of heart. May your magnificence stop me being mean. Seeing you a prodigal and open-handed giver, let me give unstintingly like a king's son, like God's own.

377
Helder Camara:
When I give food to the poor they call me a saint. When I ask why the poor have no food they call me a communist!

378
*Jim Wallis, founder of the radical Sojourners Community in Washington, USA, writing in **Call to Conversion**:*
The question to be asked is not 'What should we give to the poor?' but, 'When will we stop taking from the poor?' The poor are not our problem; we are their problem.

379
Barbara Ward, social commentator:
Christians alone straddle the whole spectrum of rich nations and therefore Christians can be a lobby of tremendous importance. When we come before our heavenly father and he says, 'Did you feed them, did you give them something to drink, did you clothe them, did you shelter them?' and we say, 'Sorry Lord, but we did give them 0.3 per cent of our gross domestic product,' I don't think that will be enough.

380
The Guardian, July 1995:
Nike pays the basketball player Michael Jordan $20 million to endorse their shoes. These used to be made in Maine, by workers charging the US average of $6.95 an hour. Today Nike favours Indonesia, where workers put in six days a week, $10^1/_2$ hours a day, and earn $37.46. At which rate, they'd equal Michael Jordan's Nike pay packet in 44,492 years.

381

Christian Aid statistics:
Each year, 114 million *Toffee Crisp* bars are made – enough to circle the equator. 3 thousand *KitKats* are eaten every minute. 283 *Smarties* are eaten every second.

A tube of *Smarties* costs roughly 32 pence. A Brazilian family working together in a cocoa plantation in Brazil earns about three pounds for a day's work.

382

John Paul Getty, multi-millionaire businessman:
The meek shall inherit the earth, but not the mineral rights.

383

*Clovis Chapell, writing in **Feminine Faces**:*
When Pompeii was being excavated, there was found a body that had been embalmed by the ashes of Vesuvius. It was that of a woman. Her feet were turned toward the city gate, but her face was turned backward toward something that lay just beyond her outstretched hands. The prize for which those frozen fingers were reaching was a bag of pearls.

Maybe she had found them where they were dropped by another. Maybe she herself had dropped them as she was fleeing for her life. But, be that as it may, though death was hard at her heels and life was beckoning beyond the city gates, she could not shake off their spell.

384

When ITV televised the morning service from Tonbridge Parish Church before Christmas, they helped the viewers by running the subtitle of the carols across the screen. One of them contained the phrase, 'Profits have spoken.' How true!

385

Newspapers are fond of giving nicknames to groups of people who are flourishing or struggling under the current economic conditions. There are:

YUPPIES: young upwardly mobile professionals;
DINKIES: double income, no kids yet;
ORCHIDS: one recent child, heavily in debt;
WOOPIES: well-off older persons;
SINBADS: single income, no boyfriend and desperate;
HOBGOBLINS: help, our budget's gone beyond the limit of our income!

386

*The **Wittenberg Door** magazine:*
A chap rang up the church office one Monday morning and asked, 'Who's the head hog at the trough?'

'Well,' gasped the secretary, 'We hardly refer to the Reverend Smith in that manner.'

The man continued, 'I don't care what you call him, I have a cheque for ten thousand dollars and I want to know where to send it. Who's the head hog at the trough?'

'Oh,' the woman chirped, 'Here comes the big pig down the corridor now.'

387

Sign outside a New Jersey convent school:
Trespassers will be prosecuted to the fullest extent of the law, Signed, The Sisters of Mercy.

And finally...

388

From the North American Cree Indian declaration:
Only when the last tree has died and the last river has been poisoned and the last fish has been caught will we realise that we cannot eat money.

Chapter 9

Suffering and sadness

389

A hermit was on ten years probation to join a silent order. At the end of a decade of monastic isolation, he was called to an interview with the chief hermit. He was allowed only two words to sum up how he felt about his progress over all that time. So he said, 'Bad food.' His superior said they would try to improve the food but further probation was required. He sent him away to pray for ten more years.

When the time was up, he was recalled for further discussion. He had thought long and hard about how to make the best use of his two words, so he said, 'Hard bed.' The superior was a sympathetic man, so he offered more help. But again, he felt that more time was required before he could fully be admitted to the order.

Ten years later, the novice found himself before the chief hermit again. This time his words were even more abrupt: 'I quit.'

The chief hermit replied, 'We decided not to accept you anyway – you've done nothing but complain ever since you arrived!'

390

The news was catastrophic! The worst fears of environmentalists were about to be realised. A great flood was going to sweep the earth, just as devastating as the one in the time of Noah. Religious leaders from around the world gathered in a symposium to discuss how to approach the crisis.

The chairman turned to the Muslim ayatollah. 'How are you advising the Islamic peoples to face this crisis?'
The ayatollah nodded seriously: 'We plan to accept our fate and die stoically, knowing it to be the will of Allah.'

The chairman then asked the pope to speak on behalf of the world's Roman Catholics: 'We are planning to pray and trust God to save us.'

Finally, the chairman invited the chief rabbi to speak. 'The Jews have lived through crises like this so many times before,' he said resignedly. 'This time we are going to learn to live under water.'

391

The Southport Visitor, January 1995:
A healing service by John Cain of Birkenhead. Owing to illness, meeting cancelled.

392

Christopher Reeve, the actor who played Superman in several movies, was asked about his wealth and his future in an American television interview:
It could happen to anybody. It is frightening how easily life can change. One moment everything is fine and then the world falls apart.

It is tragically ironic that this was one of his last interviews before a horse riding accident left him paralysed and with a broken neck.

393

John Stott, writing in Issues facing Christians Today:
I was hungry, and you formed a humanities group to discuss my hunger. I was imprisoned, and you crept off quietly to your chapel and prayed for my release. I was naked, and in your mind you debated the morality of my appearance. I was

sick, and you knelt and thanked God for your health. I was homeless, and you preached to me of the spiritual shelter of the love of God. I was lonely, and you left me alone to pray for me.

You seem so holy, so close to God. But I am still very hungry – and lonely – and cold.

394

Oscar Romero, Archbishop of El Salvador, whose outspoken and prophetic criticism of injustice led to his assassination in 1980 outside his own cathedral:
We must not seek Jesus in the pretty pictures of Christmas cribs. We must seek him among the undernourished children who have gone to bed without eating tonight, among the newsboys who will sleep covered with newspapers in doorways.

395

*Isabel Hilton, writing in the **Independent**, November 1996:*
Jaime Jaramillo is a wealthy oil man who wades through Bogata filth on rescue missions. His company includes Exxon and Chevron among its clients. But instead of living the privileged life of his class, he has chosen, for most of his adult life, to spend his time and money trying to save street children from the misery and squalor of their poverty. He says that his motivation came first from his parents, who always helped people, always gave. But he dates the beginning of his real commitment to an incident in 1973, just before Christmas.

'I was walking home when a big car passed on the street. Someone inside the car threw a toy box out. Two street children dived for the box and a little girl got to it first. She was so happy... because she was smiling at me she didn't see the truck. When it hit her she was thrown into the air... the box was not damaged at all. I picked it up. It was empty. She had died for an empty box. I knew then what I had been born to do. I went home, very angry.'

396

Gordon Wilson, who became a senator of the Republic of Ireland, was injured by a terrorist bomb in Eniskillen, Northern Ireland. His daughter Marie died:

I have lost my daughter and we shall miss her. But I bear no ill will, I bear no grudges. Dirty sort of talk is not going to bring her back to life. Don't ask me, please, for a purpose. I don't have a purpose. I don't have an answer. But I know there has to be a plan. If I didn't think that I would commit suicide. It's part of a greater plan and God is good. And we shall meet again.

397

John McVicar, ex-gangster, writing about the murder of school-children in Dunblane, Scotland, March 1996:

There are moments when you need to rest your head on holy ground ... There are times when you need religion to explain the inexplicable. Even an atheist can see there are some things you need to bow your head before.

398

John Drane, writer and theologian:

During a trip to the Philippines, I paid a visit to Smokey Mountain, a rubbish tip in Manila that is home to many thousands of people. Can you imagine a place where everything in sight is rubbish, and where people are scraping together a miserable living in 40 degree heat? No, I couldn't either. As I stood there, taking in the sights, sounds and smells, it was the nearest thing to hell that I could imagine. Tears were streaming down my face, as I realised what it really meant for people who have nothing.

And then they came. Three of them! Children of primary school age, with smiling faces and outstretched arms. Unlike every other child in Manila, they were not begging. Their hands were extended in friendship and love. As they came closer, they embraced me, as if to comfort and assure me that it was all right. Once I got a close look at them, I could see they were different. Their faces were shining with a kind of light I had never seen before. Their whole appearance some-how changed before my very eyes, and I instinctively knew they must be angels. God was in that place, after all. Why did I ever imagine it would be otherwise?

399

Found on a piece of wrapping paper beside the body of a dead child at Ravensbruck Concentration Camp, 1943:
O Lord, remember not only the men and women of good will, but those of ill will. But do not remember all the suffering they have inflicted upon us; remember the fruits we have bought thanks to the suffering – our comradeship, our loyalty, our humility, our courage, our generosity, the greatness of heart which has grown out of all this; and when they come to judgement, let all the fruits which we have borne be their forgiveness.

400

Captain Robert Scott in the journal of his last expedition to the Antarctic, 17 December 1911:
Ate the last pony today. Smith keeps our spirits up with his impressions of the Surrey XI of '07 and his tales of prole-baiting in Esher, but we all feel desperately the need of a really good, hot cup of coffee. White, no sugar, would hit the spot. Left foot has fallen off.

401

Bishop Haik Hovsepian-Mehr, chairman of the Council of Protestant Ministers in Iran, writing shortly before he was murdered in January 1994:
If we die or go to jail for our faith, we want the whole Christian world to know what is happening. We have nothing else to lose. We have tolerated all these years and kept silent. Nothing has changed. Please don't worry about me. I am ready for anything.

402

*Alexander Solzhenitsyn, writing in **The Ġulag Archipelago**:*
It was only when I lay there on rotting prison straw that I sensed within myself the first stirrings of good. Gradually it was disclosed to me that the line separating good from evil passes not through states, nor between classes, nor between political parties either, but right through every human heart ... And that is why I look back on my years in prison and say, sometimes to the astonishment of those about me: 'Bless you, prison... for having been in my life!'

(And from beyond the grave come replies: 'It is very well for you to say that when you came out of it alive!')

403

In 1820, George Baker, the Baptist minister of Wimbourne, Dorset, was distressed because his teenage son had cut himself off from the church and, as far as anyone could see, from God. The clergyman's wife became ill, suffered a great deal, and died.

Some time later his son's life took a dramatic turn, and he announced that he had come to faith in Christ. When his father asked him eagerly which sermon it was that led to the decision, he replied, 'It was the silent one my mother preached as she bore her suffering.'

404

*Karen Blixen, whose story was told in the book and film **Out of Africa**, writing under the name Isak Dinesen:*
It is a good thing to have a great sorrow. Or should human beings allow Christ to have died on the cross for the sake of their toothaches?

405

*In **One Day in the life of Ivan Denisovitch**, Alexander Solzhenitsyn portrays life in a Russian slave-labour camp. The day was utterly bleak – spartan food, hard work, primitive hygiene and cruel guards. At the end of the day the men* *retired to a vast dormitory with tiered bunk-beds. From secret hiding places in the beds many men produced little luxuries – smuggled tobacco, stolen food, photographs of loved ones:*

One man, a Baptist pastor, imprisoned for his beliefs, produced a tiny New Testament and began to read. As he did so he smiled. 'Why are you smiling?' Ivan demanded.

'Jesus commands me to ask him for daily bread,' the pastor replied. 'He has supplied my needs for today. Why shouldn't I smile?'

406

In ancient times, Spartacus was a rebel slave who raised an army and fought the massive might of the Roman legions. When his guerilla army was defeated, the Roman general faced the hordes of captured rebels, cowed in the face of mass execution, and offered them a way out. If their leader Spartacus were to give himself up, only he would be crucified. The rest would be freed.

Would Spartacus reveal his identity, one man giving himself to rescue many? There was a silence. Then, slowly, Spartacus rose to his feet. But his sacrificial gesture went unnoticed. All around him, hundreds upon hundreds of men leapt to their feet alongside him, all of them claiming: 'I am Spartacus, I am Spartacus, I am Spartacus.'

407

The rise of Hitler in 1930s Germany was accompanied by an attempt to enlist the support of the church. While many churchmen failed to foresee the evil ahead and cooperated shamefully, the Confessing Church, under Dietrich Bonhoeffer, opposed Nazism. In two thousand pulpits, preachers refused to give in to the bitter attack on all non-conformity.

In 1939 Bonhoeffer was offered a safe job in America. He turned it down and returned to confront the evil head on. Forbidden to preach or publish, he served as a double-agent on Admiral Canaris' military intelligence staff. He sought in vain the British government's support for anti-Hitler conspirators and continually challenged Christians to reject complacent, undisciplined faith. In 1943 he was arrested for smuggling fourteen Jews to safety in Switzerland and in April 1945, at the age of 39, he was executed by the Nazis.

408

Paul Claudel, French poet:
Jesus did not come to explain suffering, nor to take it away: He came to fill it with his presence.

409

Bertrand Russell, twentieth-century philosopher:
To know people well is to know their tragedy. It's usually the thing most people's lives are built around. We cry into the night and there is no reply.

410

Mother Teresa of Calcutta, founder of the Missionaries of Charity:
The hunger for love is much more difficult to remove than the hunger for bread.

411

Oscar Wilde, twentieth-century writer and wit:
How else but through a broken heart may Lord Christ enter in?

412

Henri Nouwen, Dutch Dominican and writer:
It would be just another illusion to believe that reaching out to God will free us from pain and suffering. Often, indeed, it will take us where we would rather not go. But we know that without going there we will not find our life.

413

Frances Anderson, writer:
God (but only God!) can transform evil into good, so that in retrospect (but only in retrospect!) it is seen actually to have been good, without diminishing in the least the awful actuality of the evil it was at the time.

414

*C S Lewis , writing in **The Problem of Pain**:*
God whispers to us in our pleasures, speaks in our consciences, but shouts in our pain.

415

Jürgen Moltmann, theologian:
God weeps with us so that we may one day laugh with him.

416

Adlai Stevenson, twentieth-century North American politician:
There is no evil in the atom; only in men's souls.

And finally...

417

Prince Philip, Duke of Edinburgh, writing in 1995 in the visitors' book of Yad Vesham, the holocaust museum in Jerusalem:
God brings everything we do to judgement.

Chapter 10

Hope and encouragement

418

John Henry Newman, nineteenth-century leader of the Oxford Movement, who became a Roman Catholic cardinal:
God has created me to do some definite service; he has committed some work to me which he has not committed to another. I have my mission – I may never know it in this life, but I shall be told it in the next.

I am a link in a chain, a bond of connection between persons. He has not created me for naught. I shall do good. I shall do his work. I shall be an angel of peace, a preacher of truth in my own place while not intending it, if I do but keep his commandments. Therefore I will trust him.

Whatever, wherever I am, I can never be thrown away. If I am in sickness, my sickness may serve him; in perplexity, my perplexity may serve him; if I am in sorrow, my sorrow may serve him. He does nothing in vain. He knows what he is about. He may take away my friends. He may throw me among strangers. He may make me feel desolate, make my spirit sink, hide my future from me – still he knows what he is about.

419

Julian of Norwich, fourteenth-century anchorite nun:
And these words: 'You will not be overcome,' were said very insistently and strongly, for certainty and strength against every tribulation which may come. He did not say, 'You will not be troubled, you will not be belaboured, you will not be

disquieted,' but he said, 'You will not be overcome.'

God wants us to pay attention to these words, and always to be strong in faithful trust, in well-being and in woe, for he loves and delights in us, and so he wishes us to love him and delight in him and trust greatly in him. And all shall be well. And all shall be well. And all manner of thing shall be well.

420

The Cloud of Unknowing, an anonymous fourteenth-century devotional book:
Strike that thick cloud of unknowing with the sharp dart of longing love, and on no account whatever think of giving up.

421

Betsy ten Boom, writing from Ravensbruck Nazi concentration camp:
There is no pit so deep that God is not deeper still.

422

*Minnie Louise Haskins, an extract from **God Knows**, quoted by George VI in his Christmas broadcast of 1939:*
I said to the man who stood at the gate of the year, 'Give me a light that I may tread safely into the unknown.'

And he replied, 'Go out into the darkness and put your hand into the hand of Christ. That shall be to you better than a light and safer than a known way.'

423

'Don't worry' is the most frequently repeated command in the Bible. The are 365 different occasions when the words 'do not be afraid' are used – one for each day of the year!

424

*C S Lewis' allegory **The Lion, the Witch and the Wardrobe** is set in a land of permanent, evil winter, but the approach of Aslan, who represents Jesus, changes everything:*

'Come on!' cried Mr Beaver, who was almost dancing with delight. 'Come and see! This is a nasty knock for the witch! It looks as if her power is already crumbling.'

'What do you mean, Mr Beaver?' panted Peter as they all scrambled up the steep bank of the valley together.

'Didn't I tell you that she'd made it always winter here and never Christmas? Didn't I tell you? Well just come and see!'

It was a sledge... and on the sledge sat a person whom everyone knew the moment they set eyes on him. He was a huge man in a bright red robe (bright as hollyberries) with a hood that had fur inside it and a great white beard.

'I've come at last,' said [Father Christmas]. 'She has kept me waiting for a long time, but I have got in at last. Aslan is on the move. The witch's magic is weakening.'

425

In 1953 the writer Alexander Solzhenitsyn was told he had a month to live after being diagnosed as having cancer. Since he lived at a time when his criticism of Soviet repression might have led to his work being totally destroyed, he hid it desperately. It was for this writing that he received the Nobel literature prize... seventeen years later! In The Oak and the Calf *he writes:*

With a hopelessly neglected and acutely malignant tumour, this was a divine miracle; I could see no other explanation. Since then, all the life that has been given back to me has not been mine in the full sense; it is built around a purpose.

426

Professor Sir Norman Anderson was a distinguished lawyer who spent much of his life studying the evidence for the resurrection. His Christian faith grew through a furnace of testing, notably the death of three adult children.

On one occasion, giving a *Thought for the Day* talk on Radio 4, he revealed that his son Hugh, a brilliant student at Cambridge University, had died of cancer a few days previously. Norman Anderson stated simply why he was sure that God raised Jesus from the dead. He added: 'On this I am prepared to stake my life. In this faith my son died, after saying, "I'm drawing near my Lord." I am convinced he was not mistaken.'

427
G K Chesterton, twentieth-century novelist:
Christianity had died many times and risen again; for it has a God who knew the way out of the grave ... At least five times the faith has to all appearances gone to the dog. In each of the five cases it was the dog that died.

428
Where St Paul's now stands was once an old cathedral destroyed in the great fire of London in 1666. After the fire had been extinguished, Sir Christopher Wren picked up the first stone he found from the ruins of the old building. On it was inscribed in Latin the words, 'I shall rise again.' He was to be the architect of the new cathedral. It was built in the spirit of resurrection that those words inspired and has stood to this day, through passing centuries of war and change, in the same spirit.

429
Robert Capon Farr, North American writer:
Jesus came to raise the dead. The only qualification for the gift of the gospel is to be dead. You don't have to be smart. You don't have to be good. You don't have to be wise. You don't have to be wonderful. You don't have to be anything ... you just have to be dead. That's it.

430
Martin Luther King, twentieth-century North American civil rights worker:
One day youngsters will learn words they won't understand. Children of India will ask, 'What is hunger?' Children from

Alabama will ask, 'What is racial segregation?' Children from Hiroshima will ask, 'What is the atomic bomb?'

431
*Paul Simon, from the song **Hearts and Bones**:*
The thought that life could be better is woven indelibly in our hearts and in our bones.

432
Written on a wall in the besieged Warsaw Ghetto by an unknown Jew, probably in 1943:
I believe, I believe, I believe
with a perfect faith
in the coming of the Messiah;
in the coming of the Messiah I believe.
And even though he tarry
I nevertheless believe;
Even though he tarry,
Yet, I believe in him.
I believe, I believe, I believe.

433
Gus Marwieh, African evangelist:
The devil he got a right to fight, but he ain't got no right to win.

434
Pierre Teilhard de Chardin, twentieth-century scientist and theologian:
Some day, after mastering the wind, the waves, the tides and gravity, we shall harness for God the energies of love. And then, for the second time in the history of the world, mankind will discover fire.

And finally...

435

Peter Graystone:

When I reach out my hand to the one who called himself the Way, I am reaching for the security of him who already knows and has charted each of life's bewildering paths. I may do so with utter confidence, because he holds the map.

He may lead me on paths which are not safe; he may separate me from those I love; he may take me to places where I recognise nothing. But he holds the map, and therefore I will trust him.

He may make me confused; make my spirit weary; fill me with apprehension at what the future holds. But he holds the map, and therefore I will trust him.

He may lead me to question all the things I used to be sure of; he may give me every indication of his plan for me then lead me abruptly to a closed door; he may put me through events whose significance will be a mystery until the very day I reach heaven. But he holds the map, and therefore I will trust him.

I have no idea what the road is like beyond the next turning. Let's go find out!

Chapter 11

Other points of view

436
A newspaper investigating the reliability of the best-selling books of occult lore written by Lobsang Rampa, the mystic Tibetan lama, discovered him in fact to be Cyril Hoskins, an ex-plumber from Weybridge.

437
Ramakrishna Paramahamsa, Tibetan guru:
As one can ascend to the top of a house by means of a ladder or a bamboo or a staircase or a rope, so diverse are the ways and means to approach God, and every religion in the world shows one of these ways.

438
Woody Allen, film director:
How can I believe in God when only last week I got my tongue caught in the roller of an electric typewriter?

439
Noel Coward, the twentieth-century playwright was asked, during a television interview with David Frost, whether he believed in God. He replied:
We've never been intimate!

440
Grahame Greene, twentieth-century novelist:
There's plenty in my past to confess, which would take a long time, but ... lack of belief is not something to confess. One is

sorry, but one wishes one could believe. And I pray at night that a miracle should be done and that I should believe.

441
Benjamin Jowett, nineteenth-century academic and master of Balliol College, Oxford, talking to an undergraduate who was attempting to excuse himself from early morning chapel on the grounds that he had lost his faith:
You will find God by tomorrow morning, or else leave this college.

442
Professor A J Ayer, twentieth-century philosopher:
My God, my God, I shall die a happy man if I can make one person disbelieve in God.

443
Jacques Monod, 1965 Nobel prizewinner for medicine:
The universe was not pregnant with life, nor the biosphere with man. Our number came up in a Monte Carlo game. Is it any wonder if, like the person who has just made a million at the casino, we feel strange and a little unreal?

444
In 1996 there was a series of debates in Oxford University between two famously atheistic scientists, the biologist Richard Dawkins and the chemist Peter Atkins, and a profoundly Christian theologian, Professor Keith Ward. Atkins declared, in a manner so heated that it was reported in newspapers:
It is deplorable that in modern-day Oxford the study of theology is taken so seriously that there is a professorship. You might just as well have a chair in fantasy.

445
Philip Larkin, twentieth-century poet, dismissed religion as:
A vast moth-eaten musical brocade, created to pretend we never die.

446

Martin Amis, novelist:
The entanglements of life are shapeless – just brutal happenstance, heavy-handed reality.

447

Bertrand Russell, twentieth-century philosopher:
Three passions, simple but overwhelmingly strong, have governed my life: the longing for love, the search for knowledge, and unbearable pity for the suffering of mankind.   ·

448

Someone once asked Bertrand Russell, 'Lord Russell, what will you say when you die and are brought face to face with your maker?'

He replied, 'God,' I shall say, 'God, why did you make the evidence for your existence so insufficient?'

449

Graffiti on a North London wall:
Jesus was a typical man, they always say they'll come back but you never see them again.

450

Paddy Ashdown, who grew up in Northern Ireland with a Protestant mother and Catholic father:
I do believe in a benevolent god, indeed I pray to god. But my upbringing has shown me such hatred that I no longer belong to any named, organised religion. I am a Christian, but the god I pray to is one of my own invention, one that suits me.

451

*Bob Geldof, the singer who received a knighthood for his charitable work for famine relief in Africa, in the song **This is the World Calling**:*
There's so much beauty out there, I wish I believed enough to pray.

452

From the lyric of a song by the band U2:
I believe in the kingdom come when all the colours bleed into one,
But I still haven't found what I'm looking for.

453

Ingmar Bergman, the film star who sadly did neither:
I hope I never grow so old I get religious.

454

Noel Edmonds, television personality:
The church is the dullest experience we have in this country.

455

E M Forster, twentieth-century novelist:
Poor, talkative, little Christianity.

456

Woody Allen, writing in **Remembering Needleman:**
God is silent. Now if only we can get Man to shut up!

457

Mahatma Gandhi, Indian statesman:
We would all be Christians if it were not for the Christians.

458

Jeanette Winterson, novelist:
There have been many attempts to make the Christian faith more palatable. But it can't be done. You either chuck it out as barbaric and preposterous, or you buy the whole package. Take the debate about women priests. According to the Bible you can't have women priests, and that's that. My upbringing has left me with [a formidable knowledge of the Bible]. It's rather like having a set of snakeskin luggage. People look at it in amazement, but what use is it nowadays? And it's far too heavy to carry!

459

In Peter Barnes' play *The Ruling Class,* the Earl of Gurney, a deeply disturbed man, thinks himself to be Jesus. His exasperated family ask, 'How do you know you're God?'

He replies, 'Simple! When I pray to him I find I'm talking to myself.'

460

Scientists developed a computer into which they managed, over hundreds of years, to feed the sum total of knowledge. Bloated with pride at their achievement, they asked it the ultimate question, 'Is there a god who demands our worship?'

There was a whirr inside the computer and these words appeared on the screen: 'There is now'.

461

AD 2000 *may be profoundly significant to Christians, but...*
For Muslims it will be 1420;
For Ba'hais it will be 157;
For Jews it will be 5760;
For Hindus it will be 3106.

And finally...

462

Brian Aldiss, poet, in The Path:
O Lord, in whom I've sought to disbelieve,
Look upon me;
Fortify an atheist's lack of faith,
Look upon me.

Index

Abortion 356
Acceptance 241, 321
Accidents 115
Acronyms 385
Adultery 339–341
Advent 53–56
Ageing 353–355
Alcohol 257
Ambitions 3, 129, 180
Angels 322, 398
Anger 158
Animals 216, 237
Anxiety 284, 423
Arguments 142, 143, 233
Astronomy 73, 75
Atheism 85, 444, 462
Authority 144, 176
Awe 12, 34, 44

Babies 267
Beauty 100, 292, 451
Belonging 69, 238, 269, 290
Bereavement 227
Believing 6, 9, 11, 17, 19,
  67–69, 76, 77, 82, 86, 88, 90,
  91, 95, 101, 102, 224, 396,
  426, 432, 435, 438–440, 442,
  444, 450, 451, 462
Bible 78, 293–298, 341, 405,
  458
Birds 177
Bishops 67, 137, 139–141, 143,
  144, 254
Boredom 223, 265

Body 9, 36, 316–318
Busy 226

Cats 237
Change 2, 133–135, 180, 234,
  235, 267, 430
Challenge 42, 138, 154, 189,
  240
Children 190, 191, 218,
  266–269, 311, 344, 349, 350,
  351, 356
Choices 42
Choir 262
Christians 70, 78, 123, 127,
  130, 131, 139, 141, 142, 145,
  146, 148, 149, 151–154, 182,
  231, 232, 238, 240, 241, 296,
  307, 457
Christmas 189–195, 424
Church 29, 233, 234, 236–243,
  246, 258, 259, 263–265, 269,
  279, 284, 293, 303, 304, 307,
  427, 454, 455
Cleaning 58, 303
Clergy 105, 242–251, 253–256
Comfort 57, 87, 189, 421, 426,
  429
Commitment 1, 79, 97–99, 220,
  304, 313
Communication 18
Communion 290, 291
Community 293, 313, 357, 358
Compassion 149
Complacency 119, 289, 407

Complaints 389
Compromise 234
Computers 27, 74, 185, 343, 460
Confession 112, 115, 169, 228
Conversion 70, 77, 79, 82–84, 85, 97, 112, 347, 403
Creativity 100
Creator 12–14, 21, 22, 24, 95, 183
Cross 46–49, 118, 305
Crucifixion 44, 50, 52, 53, 404

Death 51, 197–212, 216, 217, 219, 220, 222–230, 401, 429, 445
Decisions 42, 105, 435
Denominations 214, 231, 232
Despair 421, 431
Destiny 435
Difficulty 62, 70, 118, 127, 166, 433, 446
Direction 77, 107
Disability 355
Disappointment 132, 187
Doubt 5, 6, 88–90, 104, 420
Dreams 59, 213

Easter 50, 52, 121
Encouragement 133, 187, 320, 418–426, 428–433, 435
Endurance 118, 120, 124, 420
Environment 388
Epitaph 229
Eternal life 206–208, 212, 215, 216, 218, 222, 224
Euthanasia 209, 210
Evangelism 243, 244, 306, 311–313, 347
Evil 173, 236, 413, 416, 433
Evolution 6, 8
Example 43
Exams 177, 277
Excuses 313
Expectations 12, 28, 126, 131

Faith 19, 67, 76, 80, 222, 396, 432, 435, 439, 462
Fame 81, 164
Families 351, 352
Fear 34, 87, 225
Fire 59
Flood 390
Food 297
Football 80
Forgetfulness 289, 353
Forgiveness 26, 35, 45, 108–113, 218, 359, 387, 399
Freedom 26, 71, 94
Friendship 238
Future 392

Generosity 355, 367, 369, 379
Gifts 21, 61, 371
Giving 68, 291, 363, 372, 373, 375–379
God 1–29, 126, 131, 192, 261, 270, 421, 439
Good Friday 44, 49, 50
Goodness 23, 34, 402, 405, 413
Grace 45, 429
Graves 205, 207
Greed 160, 364
Guidance 80, 105–107, 422, 435
Guilt 130

Happiness 190
Hardship 70, 118, 419, 421
Healing 61, 261, 391
Heaven 206, 212–214, 217, 219, 221
Hell 219, 221, 230
Help 102, 393
Holiness 34, 308, 393
Holy Spirit 58–62, 256
Homosexuality 324
Honesty 35, 112
Hope 208, 418–425, 429, 430, 435
Hospitality 240

Humanity 19, 315–317,
320–322, 325
Humility 300
Hunger 410

Illness 117, 170
Incarnation 36, 37, 75, 302
Injustice 119, 160, 171, 380,
381
Integrity 171
Islam 248, 461

Jesus Christ 30–56, 449
Jews 390, 461
John the Baptist 314
Judgment 320, 321, 417
Justice 121, 122, 159, 161, 190,
407, 430

Kindness 68
Knowledge 22, 27, 102, 162,
177, 447

Last words 197
Leadership 178, 242
Learning 115, 144, 162
Lent 299
Lies 167
Life 165, 431, 443
Light 35, 91, 212
Listening to God 2, 144, 270,
286, 287, 456
Love 14, 15, 21, 26, 33, 49, 68,
73, 86, 89, 132, 133, 136,
221, 225, 323–328, 332, 356,
410, 434, 447

Marriage 327–334, 339, 343
Materialism 337
Maturity 145
Miracles 30, 31, 261, 270
Misprints 1, 108, 157, 254,
257, 280, 341
Mission 310, 312, 313
Missionaries 250, 307, 309
Mistakes 1, 23, 24, 108,

155–158, 191, 203, 257, 278,
280, 283, 284, 303, 307, 336,
339, 341, 346, 384
Money 359–364, 367, 372,
376, 378–380, 384–386, 388
Morality 153, 161, 172, 173,
175, 179, 334, 339–341
Motives 105, 239, 240, 255,
357, 368
Music 18

Need 16, 17, 68, 270, 290, 397
Newspapers 1, 83, 108, 138,
139
Nuns 387

Obedience 176
Opposition 120

Pain 414
Palm Sunday 300, 301
Parents 26, 186, 347–349, 351
Patience 288
Peace 430
Persecution 120
Perseverance 124, 128, 187
Pets 216
Pharisees 297
Pilgrimage 269
Politics 148, 178, 179
Pope 51
Possessions 365–372, 375, 376,
379, 382, 383
Potential 321, 431
Poverty 160, 378, 394, 398
Power 60, 144, 175, 176, 180
Prayer 48, 59, 255, 270,
271–283, 285–289, 347, 368,
393, 451, 459
Preachers 243, 249, 251
Prejudice 109, 120, 123, 241,
268
Pride 3
Priorities 81, 226, 270, 332,
361, 379
Proof 5–7, 9, 444, 448, 460

Punishment 213
Purpose 14, 21, 72, 165, 396, 402, 413, 418, 425

Questions 25, 40, 74
Quiet 270

Racism 109, 120
Reality 168
Reconciliation 142, 359
Relationships 142, 324–328, 331–335, 338, 343, 345, 346, 348, 349, 351, 352, 449
Religions 233, 248, 308, 390, 397, 436, 437, 445, 450, 453
Repentance 66, 134
Respect 308
Respectability 240, 241
Rest 215, 222
Resurrection 50–52, 121, 204, 217, 427
Riddles 65
Rights 174
Rush 286–288

Sacrifice 375, 406, 407
Sadness 397, 398, 404, 409, 411–415
Science 22, 181–184, 187, 188, 315, 316
Searching 4, 5, 10, 16, 74, 441, 452
Second Coming 55, 150, 274, 449
Self image 318
Selfishness 103, 117
Sermons 250, 252–257
Service 92, 98, 99, 126, 132, 303, 304, 309, 365, 418
Services 221, 265
Sex 330–342
Simplicity 32, 33, 73
Sin 108, 109, 111–116, 170, 173
Sport 77, 79, 80, 135
Stress 160
Submission 301

Success 81
Suffering 25, 120, 389, 390, 392–414, 418, 430, 433, 438, 447
Sunday 125
Symbols 305

Talents 80, 93
Teenagers 12, 186
Temptation 105, 114–116
Ten commandments 78, 298, 341
Thanksgiving 271, 289, 290
Time 1, 160, 288
Trinity 63–65
Trust 95, 104
Truth 101, 167

Ugliness 133
Uncertainty 5, 102, 131, 420, 422, 435
Unity 232, 238, 269, 290

Value 294
Vicars 105, 245, 247
Violence 137, 138

War 190
Water 81, 103
Wealth 200, 360, 361, 363, 371, 372, 375, 379–381, 385, 388, 395
Weddings 329, 330, 339
Welcome 240, 241, 263, 264
Wholeness 177
Witness 79, 310, 312, 347, 403
Wonder 17, 96
Work 160–164
Worry 284, 423
Worship 72, 234, 237, 239, 240, 257, 258, 260, 262, 264, 266, 292, 294, 295, 301, 302
Worth 164, 316, 319, 359, 363, 380, 388